Alexander P. Saccaro

Mein Erfolgstrainer
Englische Grammatik

Englisch 5/6

Klett Lerntraining

Bibliografische Information der Deutschen Natinalbibliothek
Die Deutsche Nationalbibliothek verzeichnet diese Publikation in der Deutschen Nationalbibliografie; detaillierte bibliografische Daten sind im Internet über http://dnb.ddb.de abrufbar.

Auflage 5. 4. 3. 2. | 2012 2011 2010 2009
Die letzten Zahlen bezeichnen jeweils die Auflage und das Jahr des Druckes.
Dieses Werk folgt der gültigen Rechtschreibung und Zeichensetzung. Ausnahmen bilden Texte, bei denen künstlerische, philologische oder lizenzrechtliche oder andere Gründe einer Änderung entgegenstehen.

www.klett.de/lernhilfen
Zeichnungen: Andreas Florian, Lübeck
Umschlaggestaltung: know idea GmbH, Freiburg, mit Franziska Döhler
Satz: Klaus Bauer, Bondorf
Reproduktion: Meyle + Müller, Medien-Management, Pforzheim
Druck: Medienhaus Plump, Rheinbreitbach
Printed in Germany
ISBN 978-3-12-927136-0

9 783129 271360

Hallo liebe Schülerin, hallo lieber Schüler!

Dein Erfolgstrainer ist genau das richtige Buch für dich,
- wenn du dich in **einem bestimmten Thema verbessern** möchtest
- wenn du dazu **Regeln, Übungen und ausführliche Lösungen** in einem einzigen Buch suchst und
- wenn du wissen willst, wie du **deinen Lernstoff zeitlich am besten einteilst**.

So erstellst du dir dein persönliches Aktiv-Lernprogramm!

Im Inhaltsverzeichnis stehen links alle Themen, die behandelt werden. Rechts werden die Themen zeitlich eingeteilt, damit du dir **dein ganz persönliches Lernprogramm** zusammenstellen kannst und dann sofort siehst, wie viel Stoff du in welcher Zeit erarbeiten kannst.

Lerneinheit: Eine Lerneinheit beträgt 20 – 30 Minuten. Das bedeutet, dass du die Übungen in dieser Zeit schaffen kannst. Aber: Das ist nur ein Richtwert. Wenn du am Anfang länger brauchst – auch kein Problem!
Eine Lerneinheit solltest du an einem Stück bearbeiten. Wenn du 2 (und mehr) Lerneinheiten machen möchtest, ist es jedoch besser, eine 10-minütige Pause dazwischen zu schieben.

Tag: Wie du im Inhaltsverzeichnis siehst, verteilen sich zusammenhängende Themen manchmal auf mehrere Tage. Versuche, an einem Thema dranzubleiben. Wenn du z. B. montags anfängst, bearbeite dienstags die nächste Lerneinheit! So bleibt am meisten hängen und du musst nicht noch mal von vorne beginnen.

Woche/Monat: Wir haben den Lernstoff zusätzlich in Wochen und Monate eingeteilt, damit du sehen kannst, wie viel Zeit du insgesamt für größere Kapitel benötigst.
So hast du immer den Überblick und bist auf den Punkt genau vorbereitet.

Wir wünschen dir viel Erfolg.

P.S. Mit deinem persönlichen Aktiv-Lernprogramm kannst du dich ohne Stress auf deine **nächsten Klassenarbeiten und Tests** vorbereiten.

1 Substantive

Weißt du noch, was Substantive bzw. Nomen *(nouns)* sind? Grob gesagt, sind es Wörter, mit denen wir Personen, Tiere, Sachen, Gegenstände und abstrakte Begriffe wie Eigenschaften und Gefühle bezeichnen. Viele dieser Substantive können im Plural gebraucht werden. Dazu musst du allerdings wissen, wie man den Plural der Substantive im Englischen bildet.

Die regelmäßige Bildung des Plurals

Im Allgemeinen bildet man den Plural im Englischen, indem man an die Singularform ein -**s** anhängt:

Singular	**Plural**
a farm	some farm**s**
a hen	some hen**s**
a sponge	some sponge**s**

Nach den Lauten [s], [ʃ], [tʃ] und [dʒ] steht ein -**es**, wenn kein -**e** im Singular vorhanden ist:

Singular	**Plural**
a bu**s**	some bus**es**
a box	some box**es**
a bush	some bush**es**
a match	some match**es**
a sandwich	some sandwich**es**

Achtung:

Auslautendes -**y** wird nach Konsonant zu -**ies**:	a bab**y**	some bab**ies**
Auslautendes -**fe** wird meist zu -**ves**:	a kni**fe**	some kni**ves**

Unregelmäßige Pluralformen

a m**a**n	two m**e**n	a f**oo**t	two f**ee**t
a wom**a**n	three wom**e**n	a g**oo**se	ten g**ee**se
a child	five child**ren**	a m**ouse**	three m**ice**

1 Mr Mason's farm

Mr Mason ist Toms Großvater. Er hat einen Hof in der Nähe von York.
Schau dir das folgende Bild an.

a) Was für Leute und welche Tiere kannst du sehen?

b) Mache dir eine Liste mit allen Substantiven. Setze die Substantive, die in der Einzahl sind, in die Mehrzahl und umgekehrt.

Beispiel: a farmhouse — some farmhouses
a wife — ______________________

2 Animals, animals ...

Wie lautet die Einzahl der folgenden Tiere, die es auf einem Bauernhof auch noch gibt?

cats	bulls	cows	dogs
horses	ponies	mice	geese

3 On Mr Mason's farm

Was kannst du für die Bilder einsetzen?

There are a lot of  __________,  __________ and  __________ on Mr Mason's farm today. They all have got  __________ for Mr Mason because it is his birthday. Look at those two  __________ over there; the big boy is Tom and the small boy is Timmy. They have got presents, too. Tom's present is a book about farms and farm animals. Timmy has got something in his  __________, too. But it is not  __________, it is only his old  __________. Poor teddy! One  __________ is missing and one  __________, too, and it is half-blind because one  __________ is gone. But Timmy has got a present for his grandad, too.

It is a wonderful picture of three big  __________. They are in the kitchen and they are eating grandpa's birthday  __________.

Merke

Bei allen Pluralformen müssen auch die Begleiter **this** und **that** in den Plural gesetzt werden:

this book – **these** books   **that** girl – **those** girls

4 Timmy's picture book

Timmy hat auch ein Buch. Er zeigt es seinem Großvater. Kannst du dir vorstellen, was Timmy seinem Großvater sagt?

1. This is a boy and these are boys, too.
2. That is a car and those are cars, too.
3. This is a street and …
4. That is a house …
5. This is a brush …
6. That is a baby …
7. This is a foot …

5 Clothes

Lies den folgenden Text und unterstreiche die Substantive im Plural.

Mr Mason is Tom's grandad. He is a farmer, but today he is not wearing his old trousers, his old shirt and his old shoes. He has got his best clothes on because it is his birthday. Mrs Mason is wearing her best clothes, too. She is not wearing her old jeans, but a nice blouse, a new skirt and some nice tights.

Merke

clothes, jeans, trousers und tights (Strumpfhose) werden im Englischen immer im Plural gebraucht. Der unbestimmte Artikel **a/an** ist vor diesen Substantiven nicht möglich.

Auch **police** und **people** werden im Englischen immer im Plural gebraucht. **Homework** steht dagegen im Englischen immer im Singular:

"Help! Where **are** the **police**?
Some **people give** us too much **homework**!"

6 Kate's clothes

Dieses Mädchen heißt Kate und ist Toms Schwester. Sieh mal, was sie anhat: Obwohl ihr Großvater Geburtstag hat, trägt sie nur alte Sachen. Kannst du die folgenden Sätze vervollständigen?

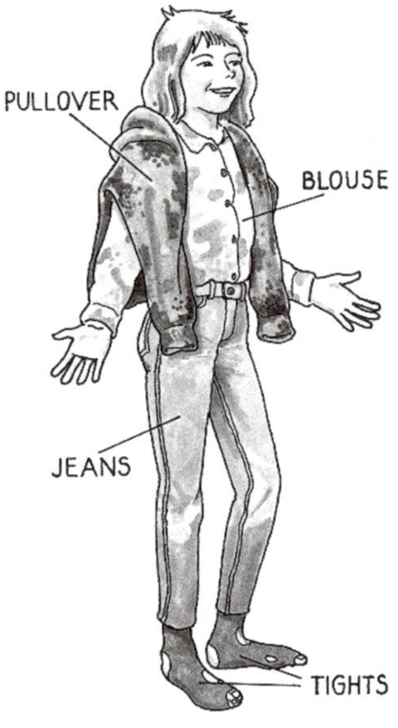

Look at her pullover.

It's dirty.

Look at her tights.

There __________ holes

in __________.

Look at her jeans.

__________ too small.

Look at her blouse.

__________ not clean.

Her clothes __________ really

awful!

7 Your clothes

a) Was hast du gerade an?

b) Welche Kleidung magst du am liebsten?

1

In Timmys Bilderbuch gibt es viele Bilder, zum Beispiel:

hens, geese, ducks, rabbits, boys, girls, children, teddies, men, women, houses, brushes, apples and sandwiches

Stelle eine Liste dieser Substantive auf. Wie lautet ihre Einzahl?

singular: a horse **plural:** some horses

2

Großmutter mag nicht, was Kate anhat. Sie fragt, weshalb Kate ihre alten Sachen trägt. Setze *it, they, them, this, these* in die folgenden Sätze ein.

Grandma: Kate, why must you wear ____________ old things?

What about ____________ old pullover, for example?

Kate: Sorry, Grandma, but my new one is in the gym.

I left ____________ there.

Grandma: And what about your jeans? ____________ are too small,

and ____________ are dirty, too.

Kate: Mum put my new ones in the washing machine.

____________ aren't dry yet.

Grandma: What about a skirt then?

Kate: I don't like skirts. We must always wear ____________ at school.

3

Herr Mason hat viele Geburtstagsgeschenke bekommen.
Vervollständige die folgenden Sätze.

There are Tom's and Timmy's presents. But there are other ____________, too.
Here is Mum's present. It's a photo album with a lot of ______________ (photo) in it. There are many ______________ (people) on them. There is another present. It's in ____________ two big ____________ (that/box) over there. What's in them? Nobody knows. And there is Kate's present, too. It's only a small present because she had too much __________________ (homework).

2 Das Personalpronomen

Pronomen stehen immer für (lat. *pro*) ein Substantiv (Nomen). Daher können sie sowohl Subjekt als auch Objekt eines Satzes sein.

Das Personalpronomen als Subjekt

Where is **Kate? She** is here. Where is **Tom? He** is at school.
Where is **your book? It** isn't here.

Ist das Personalpronomen **Subjekt** des Satzes, so lauten seine Formen:

Singular					**Plural**		
I	**you**	**he**	**she**	**it**	**we**	**you**	**they**
(ich)	(du/Sie)	(er)	(sie)	(es)	(wir)	(ihr/Sie)	(sie)

It steht immer für Sachen; **they** kann für Personen, Tiere und Sachen stehen. Alle anderen Personalpronomen stehen für Personen.

Das Personalpronomen als Objekt

Ist das Personalpronomen **Objekt** eines Satzes, lauten seine Formen:

Tom	can see	**me** (mir/mich)	**Singular**
Kate	can help	**you** (dir/dich/Ihnen)	
		him (ihm/ihn)	
		her (ihr/sie)	
		it (es)	
		us (uns)	**Plural**
		you (euch/Ihnen)	
		them (ihnen/sie)	

Im Englischen macht man bei den Pronomen keinen Unterschied zwischen dem indirekten und direkten Objekt; die Formen sind gleich. Wie bei den Subjektpronomen steht **it** für eine Sache; **them** kann für Personen, Tiere und Sachen stehen.

Die Objektform des Personalpronomens steht im Englischen auch nach Präpositionen:

Wait **for me**! Look **at her**!
Look **at him**! Wait **for them!**

1 Where are they?

Beantworte die folgenden Fragen. Verwende Personalpronomen in deinen Antworten.

1. Where is Mr Mason?	(on the farm)
2. Where's Mrs Mason?	(in the house)
3. Where's Tom ?	(at school)
4. Where's Tom's bike?	(at school, too)
5. Where's Timmy?	(on his potty)
6. Where are his toys?	(on the floor)
7. Where are his clothes?	(on his bed)
8. Where's Kate?	(not at home)
9. Where is her girlfriend?	(with her)
10. Where are Kate and Jenny?	(in the park)

2 Looking for persons and things

Beantworte die folgenden Fragen; verwende dabei Personalpronomen.

1. Where are my clothes?
2. Where is my book?
3. Where are you, Kate?
4. Where is Mike?
5. Where are Tom and Jenny?
6. Where are my CDs?
7. Where are my keys?
8. Where is my money?
9. Where is Dad?
10. Where is your potty, Timmy?
11. Where is my teddy?
12. Where are my trousers?

I can't find ...
I can't see ...
I can't hear ...

3 Looking for Timmy's toy cars

Kate ist in Timmys Zimmer. Sie sucht seine Spielzeugautos, kann sie aber nicht finden. Kannst du die Sätze vervollständigen?

Kate: Timmy, where are your toy cars? Help _________ to look for _________. Are _________ under your bed?

Timmy: No, _________ aren't. _________ aren't there.

Kate: Where are _________ then? Let _________ guess. Are _________ in your bed?

Timmy: No, _________ aren't in my bed. _________ in my teddy's bed.

Kate: In your teddy's bed? Where is _________?

Timmy: _________'s here.

Kate: But why are _________ in your teddy's bed, Timmy?

Kate: It's my teddy who wants to play with _________, not me.

1

Lehrer stellen viele Fragen. Stelle du sie einmal und gib die richtige Antwort darauf. Verwende Personalpronomen.

		in the classroom
	Tom and Mike?	here
	your homework?	on the bus
	your English book?	on the desk
Where is	your book?	at home
Where are	Christine?	not here
	the register?	in my schoolbag
	they from?	ill
	you from?	York
	Kate?	at school

2

Was musst du tun, wenn …? Beantworte die folgenden Fragen; verwende in deiner Antwort die Verben:

to read / try / wash / brush / play with /
talk to / talk about / forget / look after

Beispiel: When I've got a dog, I must look after it.

What must you do when you've got …

a dog?
a lot of homework?
dirty clothes?
a silly neighbour?
a baby?
a friend?
a new computer game?
problems?
a good book?

3 Bestimmter und unbestimmter Artikel

3.1 Der bestimmte Artikel

Wie du weißt, gibt es im Englischen nur eine Form des bestimmten Artikels *(definite article)*. Seine Aussprache richtet sich nach dem folgenden Wort. Vor einem Vokal wird *the* [ðɪː], vor einem Konsonant und dem Halbvokal [j] (wie z.B. in *unit, uniform, yellow*), wird er [ðə] ausgesprochen:

[ðɪː]	[ðə]
the **o**ther girl	the boy
the **E**nglish car	the car
the **o**ld uniform	the uniform

Wann benutze ich den bestimmten Artikel?

1. Der bestimmte Artikel steht immer, wenn es sich um bestimmte Personen oder Sachen handelt:

   The colours of Tom's school uniform are blue and grey. **The** girls must wear a grey skirt and **the** boys must wear grey trousers. **The** boys and **the** girls can wear a school blazer, too.

2. Der bestimmte Artikel steht nicht, wenn die Personen oder Sachen nicht näher bestimmt sind. Er steht daher nie bei **most** (people, girls, boys …) und **most of them**:

   Not all boys and girls in Britain like **school uniforms. Most of them** could do without a school uniform.

3. Er steht auch nicht bei Eigennamen und bei Verkehrsmitteln, wenn man sagen will, wie man irgendwo hinkommt:

   Tom goes to school **by bike.** Some children go there **by bus.**

Beachte:
Im Unterschied zum Deutschen steht der bestimmte Artikel nicht bei Straßennamen: They live **in Park Road**.

Bei Wörtern wie **bed** und **school** steht kein Artikel, wenn man ausdrücken will, was man dort tut. Ist dagegen das Möbelstück oder das Gebäude gemeint, so steht der bestimmte Artikel:

Let's go **to bed.**	Let's look **under the bed.**
Gehen wir ins Bett (= schlafen).	Sehen wir unter dem Bett nach.
He goes **to school.**	His mother is going **to the school.**
Er geht zur Schule. (= in den Unterricht)	Seine Mutter geht in die Schule (= zum Gebäude).

1 What's right?

Spricht man die folgenden Wörter mit [ðə] oder [ðɪ:]? Schreibe zwei Listen.

Beispiel: [ðə] box, [ðɪ:] empty box

_____ old women	_____ young girls	_____ American cars
_____ English children	_____ silly answers	_____ difficult questions
_____ examples	_____ bad ideas	_____ school uniforms
_____ yellow apples	_____ afternoons	_____ empty pages
_____ wrong numbers	_____ easy units	_____ terrible teachers

2 Jenny

Wo muss der bestimmte Artikel stehen, wo nicht?

Jenny isn't _____ Tom's sister, she is _____ Tom's friend. She lives in _____ Apple Street. _____ Apple Street is a small street in _____ north of _____ York. In winter she goes to _____ school by _____ bus, in summer she goes to _____ school by _____ bike. _____ Tom is in her class. She doesn't like all _____ girls and boys in her class, but she likes _____ Tom very much. She thinks he is _____ nicest boy in her class. But Jenny doesn't only like _____ Tom, she also likes _____ maths. _____ maths is _____ subject she likes best. Before _____ tests, she always helps _____ Tom.

3 How you can get there

Heute haben die Schüler Erdkunde. Sie reden in der Stunde darüber, wie sie zu anderen Städten oder Ländern reisen können. Achtung! Tom und die anderen leben nicht in Deutschland, sondern in York.

Beispiel: What about London? How can you get there? I can get there by train.

Germany – New York – Scotland – Ireland – Denmark –

France – The Isle of Wight – Wales – California

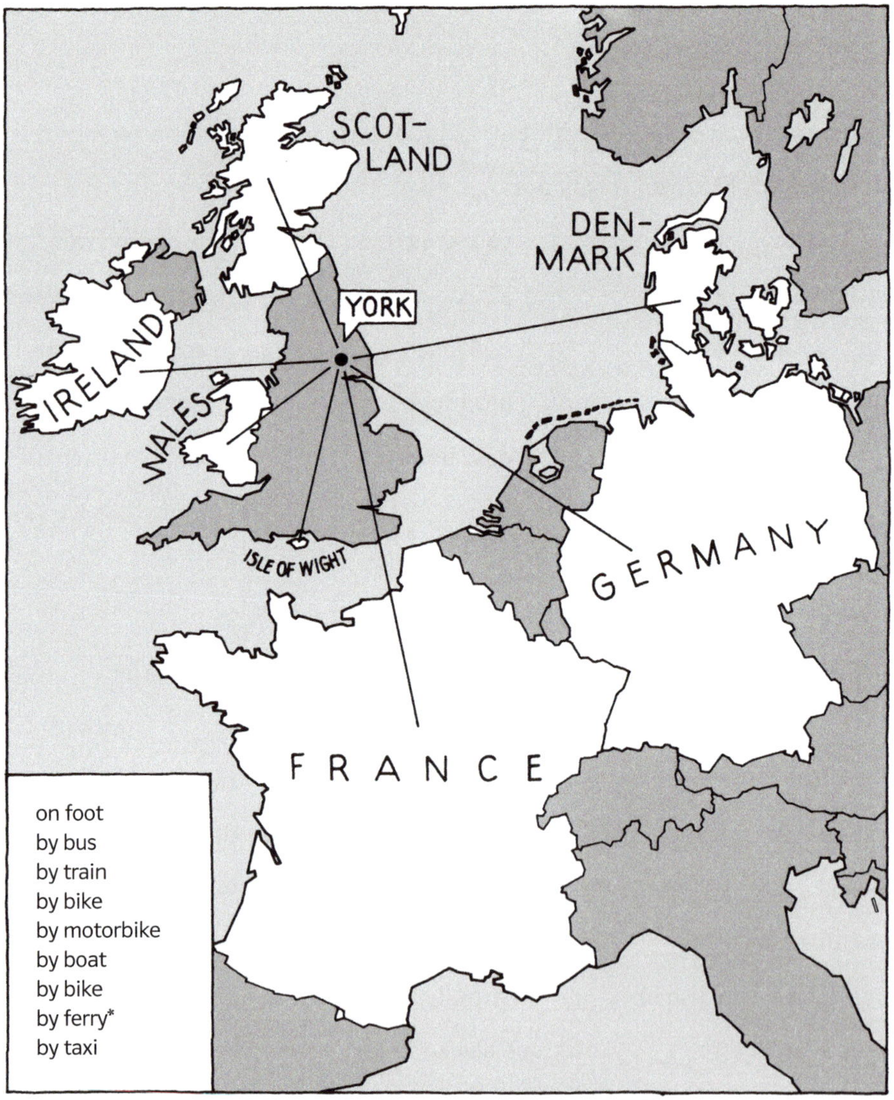

*ferry – Fähre

4 Definite article or not?

Setze den bestimmten Artikel da ein, wo er stehen muss.

1. _______ boys like _______ girls.
2. _______ Tom likes _______ Jenny.
3. Do you like _______ boys in your class?
4. Do you usually like _______ girls more than _______ boys?
5. What about _______ girls in your class? Are they nice?
6. Which of _______ boys/girls do you like best?
7. Who is _______ nicest boy/girl in your class?
8. What's _______ name of _______ girl/boy you like best?
9. Which boy/girl do _______ most of you like best?
10. Are _______ girls/boys in your class good at English?
11. Are _______ boys as clever as _______ girls? What do you think?

3.2 Der unbestimmte Artikel

Der unbestimmte Artikel bezeichnet einzelne Personen oder Dinge. Er hat im Englischen zwei Formen: *a* und *an*. Vor einem Vokal steht *an*, vor einem Konsonant und vor dem Halbvokal [j] (wie in *unit, uniform, yellow*) steht *a*.

a book	**an a**pple
a good book	**an E**nglish book
a yellow car	**an e**mpty car
a nice uncle	**an u**ncle
a uniform	**an o**ld uniform

Wann benutze ich den unbestimmten Artikel?

Im Unterschied zum Deutschen steht der unbestimmte Artikel im Englischen bei Berufsbezeichnungen und bei bestimmten Ausdrücken wie *to have (got) a headache/a temperature* (Kopfweh, Fieber haben):

Tom has got **a** new girlfriend.
Her father is **a** taxi driver.
She's ill today; she's got **a headache** and **a temperature**.

5 Tom's school bag

Packst du deinen Schulranzen jeden Tag neu? Tom tut es nicht.

There are lots of things in Tom's school bag; there's  _____ English book,  _____ workbook,  _____ exercise book,  _____ German book and  _____ pencil case in it.

But there are other things, too. There's  _____ apple,  _____ empty bottle,  _____ water pistol and  _____ old sandwich in it.

6 Who are they?

1. He brings the milk in the morning. *He's a milkman.*
2. He brings you letters and parcels. He's ____________________
3. You go to him when you want to buy sausages. ____________________
4. He sells you all kind of vegetables. ____________________
5. She helps you to find what you want when you are in a shop.

   ____
6. She works for a newspaper. ____________________
7. He comes when your house is on fire. ____________________
8. He helps animals when they are ill. ____________________
9. He gives you good or bad marks. ____________________
10. He breaks into your house to steal something. ____________________

7 More persons and things

Setze alles in die Einzahl. Verwende *a* oder *an*.

Beispiel: an old woman, a young girl

_____ old women	_____ young girls	_____ American cars
_____ English children	_____ silly answers	_____ difficult questions
_____ examples	_____ bad ideas	_____ school uniforms
_____ yellow apples	_____ afternoons	_____ empty pages
_____ wrong numbers	_____ easy units	_____ terrible teachers

8 Jenny is ill

Steht hier der bestimmte, der unbestimmte oder gar kein Artikel?

Jenny goes to __________ same school as __________ Tom. Sometimes Tom's father takes them to __________ school in __________ morning. __________ school they go to is __________ big school. There are a lot of __________ pupils at Jenny's school, and not all of them like __________ school. But Jenny does; she likes __________ school because __________ most of __________ teachers she has got are really nice. Today she can't go to __________ school; she must stay in __________ bed, but she hasn't got __________ temperature. She's got __________ cold and __________ bad headache. She feels terrible and she doesn't want to eat anything. She just wants to see __________ doctor and stay in __________ bed. Poor Jenny!

1

Bestimmter, unbestimmter oder gar kein Artikel? Was ist richtig?

Tom has got _______ brother and _______ sister. They live in _______ York. That's in the north of _______ England. _______ Timmy is his baby brother and Kate is his sister.

Tom has got _______ grandpa and _______ grandma, too. His grandfather's name is Mr Mason. He has got _______ farm, so he is _______ farmer.

Tom and Kate go to _______ school, but Timmy doesn't. He's too young to go to _______ school. It's sometimes hard for Tom and Kate to get out of _______ bed when Timmy can still stay in it.

Tom usually goes to school by _______ bike. He only takes _______ bus when it's too cold or too windy. Kate goes to school by _______ bus. She mustn't go _______ bike; her mother says she is too young. Tom and Kate don't like everything about _______ school, but _______ most of their teachers are nice.

2

Schreibe ein paar Zeilen über dich selbst und deine Familie.

- where you live
- what street or road you live in
- how old you are
- if you've got a brother or a sister
- if you've got a boyfriend/girlfriend
- what your father's and mother's job is
- if and why you like or don't like school
- what subject you like best
- what subject you hate
- if your teachers are okay or not
- how you get to school in summer/winter
- what you like better
- how your father and mother go to work

4 Substantive und ihre Begleiter

4.1 Die Possessivbegleiter

Englische wie deutsche Substantive stehen nicht immer allein. Sie werden häufig von anderen Wörtern „begleitet", die sie näher bestimmen. In der deutschen Grammatik nennt man diese Wörter „Begleiter"; in der englischen Grammatik heißen sie *determiners*.

Die Possessivbegleiter *my, your* usw. drücken Besitz oder Zugehörigkeit aus. Mit Ausnahme von *their*, das sich auch auf Sachen beziehen kann, beziehen sich *my, your* usw. immer auf Personen.

Die Formen der Possessivbegleiter *(possessive determiners)* lauten:

	Singular	
This isn't	**my**	book.
Is it	**your**	book?
No, it isn't. It's	**her**	book.
No, it's	**his**	book.

	Plural	
Oh no. Is it	**your**	book, Tom and Kevin?
Let's see. No, it isn't	**our**	book. Perhaps it's the girls' book.
Yes, it is. It's	**their**	book.

Neben diesen Formen kommt auch *its* vor. *Its* bezieht sich immer auf eine Sache:

This is our school. **Its** classrooms are very nice.
This is Tom's bike. **Its** saddle is new.

1 Everybody has got something

Verwende die Possessivbegleiter.

Beispiel: Timmy has got a teddy. It's his teddy.

1. The Masons have got a flat. ____________________
2. Mr and Mrs Mason have got a car. ____________________
3. Tom has got a sister. ____________________
4. Kate has got a brother. ____________________
5. Timmy has got a lot of toys. ____________________
6. Mike has got a camera. ____________________
7. Jenny has got a boyfriend. ____________________
8. Jenny and Tom go to the same school. ____________________
9. Jenny's parents have got a house. ____________________

2 Timmy's "toys"

Jüngere Geschwister „finden" manchmal Dinge, die ihnen nicht gehören. Das ist auch bei Timmy so. Vervollständige, was seine Mutter sagt.

1. What have you got here, Timmy? What about these keys? Aren't they Dad's keys? I think they are ________ keys.
2. Look, Timmy, it's not ________ exercise book, it's Kate's. It's ________ exercise book.
3. Where have you got that from, Timmy?! Jenny's German book! How can Jenny do German tests when you keep it under ________ bed? What will ________ teacher say?
4. And look, Timmy. This is not ________ picture book. It's Kate's. It was ________ birthday present from Tom. So you can't keep it.
5. Don't cry, Timmy. Look, you've got so many things: Here's ________ teddy, here's ________ toy car, here's ________ telephone. So play with ________ things now.

Verwechsle nicht **you** mit **your**, **its** mit **it's**, **they** mit **their** und **they're** mit **there**!

1. **your, its, their** stehen nie allein. Sie stehen **immer vor** einem Substantiv.
3. **they** ist ein Personalpronomen und **steht für** ein Substantiv im Plural. **they're** ist die Kurzform von **they are**.
3. **there** (= da, dort, dahin, dorthin) steht entweder allein oder vor einer Form von *to be* (= es gibt, es sind). Nach **there is** muss das Substantiv im Singular stehen; nach **there are** folgt ein Substantiv im Plural:

   There **is a boy** over there and there **are some girls** there, too.

Vergleiche:

Timmy, where are **you**?
Where is **your** teddy?
It's Tom's bike. **Its** saddle is new. **It's** got a new bell, too.
Are Tom and Mike **there**? No, **they** aren't. **They're** at school.
Where are **their** bikes? **They're** over **there**.

3 Questions, questions …

Setze *you* oder *your* ein und beantworte dann die Fragen.

1. What about ________ room? Do ________ like it?
2. Do ________ clean it or does ________ mother clean it?
3. What's in ________ room?
4. Is there anything under ________ bed?
5. Where do ________ keep ________ clothes?
6. Where do ________ do ________ homework?
7. Have ________ got a TV in ________ room?
8. Have ________ got posters and photos in ________ room, too?

4 Tom's room

Füge *its, it's, they, their* oder *there* ein.

__________ are a lot of things in Tom's room. __________ are books and CDs everywhere. __________ are on the chairs, on his bed and on the floor. And __________ is something under his bed. What is it? __________ an old pullover. __________ are some socks under his bed, too. __________ are holes in them and __________ look dirty. And what's that on the wall? __________ are a lot of photos and posters on the wall over his bed. Look at that photo over __________. __________ a photo of Jenny. She is sitting on her bike. __________ not a new bike, but __________ handlebars and __________ saddle are new.

5 A classroom

Beschreibe dieses Klassenzimmer. Verwende *there is, there are* in deinen Sätzen.

4.2 Die Demonstrativbegleiter

Die Demonstrativbegleiter *(demonstrative determiners) this/these* verweisen auf Personen oder Dinge, die in der Nähe des Sprechers sind; *that/those* verweisen dagegen auf Personen oder Dinge, die weiter entfernt sind.

Look at **this** book. **This** isn't my book.
And what about **that** book over there? Yes, **that's** my book.
And what about **these** pencils? Aren't they your pencils?
No, they aren't. But give me **those** pencils over there. They may be my pencils.

Ob du *this/that* oder *these/those* verwenden musst, hängt auch von dem folgenden Substantiv ab. Steht das Substantiv im Singular, steht immer *this/that*; steht das Substantiv im Plural, steht immer *these/those*.

This is my book and **that** is your book.
These are my pencils and **those** are your pencils.

6 Timmy at school

Heute muss Frau Mason zum Arzt gehen. Da auch Herr Mason nicht zu Hause bleiben kann, nimmt Tom seinen kleinen Bruder in die Schule mit. Dort will Timmy alles wissen. Setze *this* oder *that* ein.

Timmy: Is ____________ your classroom, Tom?

Tom: No Timmy, ____________ isn't my classroom. My classroom is over there.

Timmy: Is ____________ your class, Tom?

Tom: Yes, ____________ is my class.

Timmy: And ____________ class over there?

Tom: ____________'s Kate's class.

Timmy: Is ____________ your chair here?

Tom: Yes, it is. And look, Timmy, ____________ chair over there, that's Jenny's.

Timmy: What's the name of ____________ fat boy over there?

Tom: His name is John, but don't call him fat because he doesn't like it.

Timmy: Is ____________ a teacher over there, Tom?

Tom: No, it isn't. It's a pupil, Timmy.

Timmy: But ____________ is a teacher, Tom.

Tom: Where? Over there? Oh yes, ____________'s our English teacher. You're right, Timmy.

Timmy: And the girl beside him is his daughter?

Tom: No, Timmy, it isn't. It's a girl in Kate's class.

7 A pupil's work

In diesem Text gibt es 15 Fehler. Kannst du sie finden? Schreibe den Text noch mal, aber jetzt ohne Fehler.

This is my classroom. Their is room for 30 pupils. Their are 30 chairs and 15 desks in it and their is a desk and a chair for our teachers, too. Its a nice room. Their are many pictures on the walls and their is a map of England, too. Its on the back, over their. The desk in front of the teacher's desk is my desk. My friend sits their. This is okay, but behind me, their are two girls ... I don't like they. They always talk and throw things at my and my friend. And when they are quiet, they eat there sandwhiches and there chocolate pudding and there sweets. They ...

4.3 *much* und *many*

Zu den Substantivbegleitern zählen auch *much* und *many*. Beide entsprechen, wenn sie vor einem Substantiv stehen, dem Deutschen „viel(e)". *Much* und *many* werden jedoch unterschiedlich gebraucht.

1. **many** kann nur bei einem Substantiv im Plural stehen:

   Are there **many girls** in your class? **How many teachers** have you got? How **many** tests do you have a week?

2. **much** steht nur bei einem Substantiv im Singular:

   How much homework do you get? **How much time** do you spend on your homework?

3. Bezieht sich **much** auf ein Verb, so bedeutet es meistens „sehr":

   Do you like **English** very **much**?

8 A questionnaire

Füge *much* oder *many* ein.

1. How ___________ homework have you got today?
2. How ___________ time do you usually spend on it?
3. How ___________ minutes do you spend on your English homework?
4. How ___________ hours do you spend in front of the TV?
5. How ___________ subjects have you got?
6. How ___________ help do you get from your parents?
7. How ___________ tests do you have a year?
8. How ___________ good marks did you get last year?
9. How ___________ tests have you written this week?

4.4 *Some* und *any*

Zu den Substantivbegleitern gehören auch *some* und *any*. Sie geben unbestimmte Mengen an. Ihre genaue Bedeutung hängt jedoch von der Satzart und dem folgenden Substantiv ab:

Kate needs **some** money.	(etwas)
She must buy **some** exercise-books.	(einige, ein paar)
But she doesn**'t** have **any** money.	(kein)
So she ca**n't** buy **any** exercise-books.	(keine)
So she asks Tom:	
Have you got **any** money?	(----)
Or have you got **any** exercise-books for me?	(irgendwelche)

Some steht in bejahten Sätzen, *any* in Fragen. *Not … any* steht dagegen in verneinten Sätzen.

Not … any entspricht dem Deutschen „kein/ eine“. In dieser Bedeutung kann es durch ***no*** ersetzt werden.

Achtung:
Als Subjekt eines Satzes ist *not ... any* nicht möglich. Hier musst du *no* + Substantiv gebrauchen.

9 No food today …

a) Setze *some* und *any* ein.

When Tom comes home from school, he is always hungry. Usually there is _________ food for him in the fridge, but today it is empty. There is nothing in it. There isn't _________ butter, there isn't _________ bread, there isn't _________ jam or marmalade left. And there isn't _________ milk and _________ orange juice in it *either. But there is a piece of paper on the table with _________ money on it. It reads: Sorry Tom, you must do the shopping today. There are _________ people waiting for me in my office. Buy yourself _________ food and buy _________ milk, too. And buy _________ orange

*not … either – auch nicht

juice for your sister. I hope the money is enough. Have you still got ________ left ? Then take it. I must go to my bank first. See you later. Mum

b) Setze *no* ein, wo dies möglich ist.

10 Shopping

Vervollständige mit *some* oder *any*.

Before Tom goes shopping, he asks himself (= sich):

What am I going to eat? Some sausages perhaps? No, I won't have ________ sausages today. I had sausages yesterday.

An omelette then? Okay, but then I need three eggs and ________ milk. Are there ________ eggs left? Let me see. Yes, there are ________ eggs in the fridge.

And what about milk? Mum says that I must buy ________. Then I'll buy ________.

Do I need ________ thing else? ________ peas perhaps?

Have I got everything? Let's see ... Oh, the money, of course. Where is my money? Oh yes, there's ________ money in my pocket. Is it enough? Yes, it is. Then I can buy ________ bottles of coke and ________ other things, too!

1

Trage in den Lehrerfragen ein, was fehlt.

a) Well, let me see ________ homework, John. Is this ________ homework or is it Kevin's homework? But why don't ________ tell me that ________ couldn't do it?

b) Where is ________ homework, Barbara? Can ________ show me ________ exercise book?

c) And what about ________, Tom and Jenny? What are ________ doing over there? Are ________ copying ________ neighbours' homework?

2

Ergänze mit *this / that* und den entsprechenden Pluralformen.

1. Is ________ your pencil-case Tom? No, it isn't. My pencil-case is over there.
2. What about ________ girls over there? Do you know them?
3. Yes, I know them. ________ girl is my sister and ________ girl is Jenny.
4. And the girl over there? Is ________ your girlfriend? No, silly, it isn't.

3

Übersetze bitte.

I've got __________ (viel Zeit), __________ (viele Freunde), __________ (viele Bücher), __________ (viel Spaß), but I haven't got __________ (viel Geld).

4

Setze *some*, *any* oder *no* ein.

Do you know ________ pupils who have got problems at home? Well, I know ________. ________ of them have got really big problems. Kevin, for example, hasn't got ________ parents. And Jim's parents have got little or ________ money and Jim's mother is often ill. From time to time she must stay in hospital for ________ weeks.

5 Der Genitiv

5.1 Der *s*-Genitiv

Im Englischen gibt es zwei Möglichkeiten, den Genitiv zu bilden: den *s*-Genitiv *(s-genitive)* und den *of*-Genitiv *(of-genitive* oder *of-phrase)*.

Der *s*-Genitiv steht zumeist bei Personen. Wie die Possessivbegleiter *my, your* usw. gibt er an, wem etwas gehört oder wem etwas zuzuordnen ist.

Die Formen des *s*-Genitiv

Singular: …'s	Kate**'s** book a child**'s** voice
Regelmäßiger Plural: …s'	the girl**s'** books my parent**s'** house
Unregelmäßiger Plural: …'s	children**'s** voices people**'s** ideas

Achtung:
Verwechsle den *s*-Genitiv nicht mit dem Plural-s. Beim Plural steht **nie** ein Apostroph!

My **parents** are not at home.

Auch bei der 3. Person Einzahl im *simple present* steht nie ein Apostroph.

He **works** in an office.

Verwechsle den *s*-Genitiv auch nicht mit den Kurzformen von *is* und *has*.

He's got a house. **It's** new.

1 The s-genitive

Bilde den *s*-Genitiv.

Beispiel: Timmy's toys

Timmy
toys

the boys
teacher

the girls
school bags

our cat
food

Kate
friends

women
clothes

the man
boots

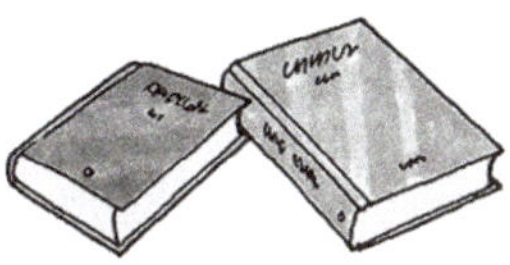

the children
books

girls
school uniforms

Jenny
dog

the Masons
house

my parents
car

2 A dialogue

Stelle die Fragen und beantworte sie.

Beispiel: Are these your books, Mike? No, they aren't. They are Peter's.

Is this your … / Are these your …

… toys, Tom?	No, ______________________	(baby brother)
… girlfriend, Kevin?	No, ______________________	(Tom)
… magazine, Jenny?	No, ______________________	(the girls)
… cat, Kate?	No, ______________________	(my mother)
… homework, Joe?	No, ______________________	(Kevin)
… house, Mr Mason?	No, ______________________	(grandparents)
… your bike, Mrs Mason?	No, ______________________	(Kate)
… your room, Tom?	No, ______________________	(my sister)
… your teddy, Jenny?	No, ______________________	(Timmy)
… your van, Timmy?	Yes, it is. It's my van!	

3 Timmy's treasures

Trage das fehlende Genitiv-s, das fehlende Plural-s, die fehlenden Apostrophe und Kurzformen ein.

Timmy is Tom_____ baby brother. He is three years old. One of his favourite toy_____ is his teddy; but he_____ got other toy_____, too. He keeps them in his cupboard; but there are other thing_____ in his cupboard. Look! There_____ one of Jenny_____ letter_____ to Tom; there_____ an old German book and there_____ Kate_____ ruler. There are also some key_____; are they his parent_____ key_____? There_____ a tennis ball, too. Whose is it? Is it Kevin_____ or Joe_______? It can't be Kate_____ or Tom_____ because they don't play tennis.

4 Jenny

Nimm zwei verschiedene Farbstifte und unterstreiche – jeweils in einer anderen Farbe – die *s*-Genitive und die Kurzformen, die du hier findest.

Jenny is Tom's girlfriend. She's twelve. She hasn't got a brother or a sister; she's only got her parents. Jenny is from York; her mother is from York, too, but her father is from Nottingham. They live in an old house; it's her grandparents' house. Jenny's other relatives live in London; she's got an aunt there who's over sixty and who's got a flat in London. She hasn't got any children, so Jenny is her only niece. In her summer holidays Jenny wants to see her: it will be Jenny's first visit to London.

5.2 Der *of*-Genitiv

Der ***of***-Genitiv drückt Zugehörigkeit und Mengenangaben aus. Im Unterschied zum ***s***-Genitiv steht er meist nur bei Sachen.

Zugehörigkeit	**Mengenangaben**
the pages **of** a book	a bottle **of** lemonade
the legs **of** the table	a pound **of** apples

5 The of- or s-genitive?

Was ist richtig?

Beispiel: the boys' legs – the doors of my room

the boys/legs	the hands/girl	the car/windows
the doors/my room	the dog/feet	my neighbour/cat
Kate/books	the children/clothes	the end/school
on the evening/my birthday	the light/the moon	Jenny/story

6 What goes together?

Bilde Paare.

Beispiel: a bar of chocolate

a bar	milk	a tin	cornflakes
lots	tea	a pound	crisps
a glass	food	a bag	cheese
a cup	strawberries	a packet	peas
a plate	chocolate	a plate	sausages

7 Tom's shopping list

In ein paar Tagen hat Tom Geburtstag. Er möchte ein paar Freunde einladen und eine Party geben. Am Tag vor der Party geht er in ein Geschäft, um einzukaufen. Hier ist seine Einkaufsliste. Kannst du sie vervollständigen?

five ______________________ *crisps*

three ______________________ *biscuits*

five ______________________ *coke*

five ______________________ *lemonade*

a ______________________ *tomato ketchup*

three ______________________ *sausages*

five ______________________ *ice cream*

8 In the shop

Tom ist jetzt im Laden. Mrs White hilft ihm. Kannst du aufschreiben, was sie wohl sagen?

Mrs White: What can I do for you, Tom?

Tom: Can I have some crisps and some biscuits?

Mrs White: How many packets do you need?

Tom: I need three ________________ and five ________________.

Mrs White: Here you are. Anything else, dear?

Tom: I need some coke and some lemonade, too.

Mrs White: ____

____

Tom: ____

____

Schau dir den Einkaufszettel in Aufgabe 7 an und setze das Gespräch fort.

1. Der ***of***-Genitiv wird oft mit der Präposition **off** (von … herunter/weg) oder mit **out of** (aus/heraus) verwechselt:

   Tom takes some money **out of** his purse.
   The purse falls **off** the table. Hands **off**! It's Tom**'s** purse. It's one **of** his birthday presents.

2. Verwechsle den ***of***- und den **s**-Genitiv nicht mit der Präposition **from.** Die Präposition **from** gibt meist eine Richtung von einer Person oder von einem Ort her an:

   I've got a postcard **from** my father. It's **from** London.
   There are greetings **from** all the family on it.

9 The s-genitive, *of, out of, off* or *from*?

Ergänze.

"Get _________ that bike," Tom says to Mike. "Let's put all the things on it. Then we needn't carry them." So they put all their things on Tom_____ bike. " "Be careful, Mike, hold the bottles or they will fall _________ the bike." So Mike takes one hand _________ his pockets and tries to hold them. It is not very far _________ the corner shop to the Masons_____ flat. But soon there is a loud crash and the bottles fall _________ the bike. Two bottles _________ lemonade are broken. So they have to go back to Mrs White_____ shop. This time they get home all right. Mike takes both hands _________ his pockets and no bottles fall _________ the bike. At home, they carry everything into the kitchen. Then they go upstairs into Tom_____ room and talk about the party. Five minutes later there is a phone call _________ Jenny_____ mother. "Jenny is ill, Tom. She's just come home _________ school and she looks really ill. I'm afraid she can't come to your party. But she will ring you up later; you will hear _________ her tomorrow. Bye, Tom, and have a nice party!"

1

Benutze den *of*- oder den *s*-Genitiv. Bilde mindestens 12 Paare.

Tom	milk	biscuits	legs
a packet	lemonade	my parents	comics
a bucket	computer	the legs	things
a pound	Jenny	the children	string
Timmy	trousers	magazines	people
a list	room	women	place

2

In den folgenden Sätzen gibt es einige Fehler. Kannst du sie verbessern?

Do you like birthday parties? I like them. There are always lots of people's there. You can play games' and theres always some kind off fun. I hope Toms birthday party will be funny, too. There are some people's I know, too: Theres Jenny, theres Ann and theres his sister Kate, too. And perhaps Betty will be there, too. Shes a very nice girl, not as silly as the other girl's …

3

Füge *out of, off, from, of* ein.

a) This plane is taking __________.

b) This is a letter __________ London. It's __________ Jenny's aunt.

c) This boy is taking __________ his clothes. He's taking the money __________ his pocket.

d) Where are you __________?

e) Turn the lights __________, please.

f) Is this one __________ your jokes?

6 *Have got, has got* und das *simple present*

6.1 *Have got* und *has got*

Ob du *have got* oder *has got* verwenden musst, hängt vom Subjekt des Satzes ab:

Kate has got a bike.
My friends have got bikes, too.

Meist werden die Kurzformen verwendet, und zwar sowohl in bejahten als auch in verneinten Sätzen:

I've got a lot of books. **I haven't got** a pet.
Tom's got a baby brother. **He hasn't got** a baby sister.

Beachte:
has steht nur in der 3. Person Singular.
Bei **haven't** fällt das **-e** nicht aus. Der Apostroph steht hier für das ausgefallene „o“ von *not*. Bei **has** steht nie ein **-e**.

Wie verwende ich *have got* und *has got* in Fragen und Kurzantworten?

1. Bei Fragen stehen *have/has* vor dem Subjekt, *got* steht nach dem Subjekt.
2. Bei Kurzantworten musst du das Subjekt als Pronomen wiederholen.
3. Nach *yes* steht eine bejahte Langform, nach *no* eine verneinte Kurzform.
4. In der Kurzantwort steht kein *got*.

Has Kate got a brother? Yes, **she has**.
Has Kate got a sister? No, **she hasn't**.
Have her parents got a house? No, **they haven't**.
Have they got a flat? Yes, **they have**.

1 The Masons' home

Füge die Formen von *have got* ein.

1. Tom's parents live in York. They ________________ a flat there.
2. Tom ________________ a room, and Kate ________________ a room, too.
3. Timmy ________________ a room. He is too young.
4. The Masons ________________ a car.
5. Tom and Kate ________________ a car,
   they ________________ bikes.
6. Timmy ________________ a bike because he's too young.
7. But he ________________ two big toy cars and other toys in his room.

2 What Kate has got

Bilde Sätze.

Beispiele:
1. Kate has got two brothers, but she hasn't got a sister.
2. What about you? I have got …, but I haven't got … .
3. What about your friend(s)? Have they got brothers, sisters, etc?

two brothers	~~boyfriend~~	bike	books	a football	a radio
~~sister~~	a lot of friends	~~car~~	~~toy car~~	~~dog~~	~~TV set~~

3 What about you? What have you got?

Stelle Fragen und gib die entsprechenden Kurzantworten.

Has Have	you your parents your friends your mother your grandmother your English teacher your boyfriend your father	got got	a car a lot of toys a computer a water pistol computer games a toy car a lot of friends a hamster	?	Yes, … No, …

6.2 Das *simple present* von *to be*

Bejahte Formen		**Verneinte Formen**	
Langformen	Kurzformen	Langformen	Kurzformen
I **am**	I'**m**	I **am** not	I'**m not**
you **are**	you'**re**	you **are** not	you **aren't**
he **is**	he'**s**	he **is** not	he **isn't**
she **is**	she'**s**	she **is** not	she **isn't**
it **is**	it'**s**	it **is** not	it **isn't**
we **are**	we'**re**	we **are** not	we **aren't**
you **are**	you'**re**	you **are** not	you **aren't**
they **are**	they'**re**	they **are** not	they **aren't**

Auch bei **to be** richtet sich die Form des Verbs nach dem Subjekt des Satzes:

I	**am**	ill.
They	**are**	my friends.

4 Tom's birthday

Füge die Formen von *to be* ein.

Today, it _______ Tom's birthday. He _______ twelve years old today. All his friends _______ there. His sister _______ there, too. Her name _______ Kate. Only Jenny _______ not there. Where _______ she? She _______ ill. All the children _______ in the kitchen; it _______ full of children. They _______ all hungry and thirsty. There _______ a lot of sandwiches on the table; there _______ some bottles of lemonade, too. But one bottle _______ on the floor; it _______ broken and there _______ a pool of lemonade around it. And who _______ in the pool? It _______ Timmy, Tom's baby brother.

Wie verwende ich *to be* in Fragen und Kurzantworten?

- Bei Fragen mit **to be** steht das Verb vor dem Subjekt.
- Bei Kurzantworten, die sich im Deutschen auf „Ja" oder „Nein" beschränken, musst du im Englischen das Subjekt als Pronomen wiederholen.
- Bei einer Antwort mit *yes* steht das Verb in der Langform, bei *no* in der Kurzform.

  Is it Kate's birthday? No, it **isn't**.
  Is Jenny there, too? No, she **isn't**.
  Is she ill? Yes, she **is**.
  Are Tom and Jenny unhappy? No, they **aren't**.
  Are the children hungry? Yes, they **are**.

- Bei Fragen mit **is there/are there** ist **there** das Subjekt der Frage und muss in der Kurzantwort wiederholt werden:

  Are there sandwiches on the table? Yes, **there are**.
  Is there a bottle on the floor? Yes, **there is**.

- Auf die Frage **is that** antwortet man mit **Yes, it is/No, it isn't**, auch wenn nach Personen gefragt wird:

  Is **that** Tom's baby brother? Yes, **it is**.

5 Tom's birthday

Lies noch einmal die Aufgabe 4 durch und gib dann Kurzantworten.

nochmal

1. Is it Timmy's birthday?
2. Is Jenny there?
3. Is Tom eleven years old?
4. Is Jenny Tom's mother?
5. Is Kate Tom's sister?
6. Is that Timmy in the pool of lemonade?
7. Are there sandwiches on the table?
8. Are the children in the bathroom?
9. Are they hungry and thirsty?
10. Is one bottle on the floor?

6.3 Der Gebrauch von *to be* in Fragen mit Fragewörtern

Das *simple present* von *to be* wird häufig in Fragen verwendet, die mit einem Fragewort beginnen. Die Fragewörter werden vor die Form von *to be* gestellt. Die übrige Wortstellung ändert sich nicht.

Who is Jenny?	**who** (= wer) fragt nach Personen.
What is on the table?	**what** (= was) fragt nach Sachen.
Where is Jenny?	**where** (= wo) fragt nach einem Ort.
Why isn't Jenny here?	**why** (= warum) fragt nach dem Grund.
How old is she?	**How** (= wie) fragt nach der Art und Weise und in Verbindung mit *old* nach dem Alter.

6 Who or where?

Was ist richtig?

1. ______________ is Timmy? He's Tom's baby brother.
2. ______________ is he? He's at Tom's party.
3. ______________ is Mike from? He's is from Bristol.
4. ______________ is Bristol? It's in England.
5. ______________ is Jenny? She's Tom's friend.
6. ______________ is she? She's at home.
7. ______________ are Joe and Kevin? They are in the kitchen.

7 Jenny

Auf der Party möchte Mike alles über Jenny wissen. Er stellt Tom eine Menge Fragen. Kannst du seine Fragen aufschreiben?

- who Jenny is
- if she is from York
- why she isn't here
- if her parents are at home
- how old she is
- if she is often ill

1

Vervollständige die Sätze mit den Formen von *to be* und von *have got*.

a) This ______________ Kevin and that ______________ Joe.

b) They ______________ the best friends I ______________.

c) And that boy over there ______________ Bill.

d) He ______________ in my class, too, and he ______________ very good at maths.

e) And this ______________ Ann. She ______________ Jenny's friend.

f) She ______________ very sorry that Jenny can't ______________ here.

2

Auf Toms Party spielen die Schüler ein Spiel. Tom denkt an seinen Englischlehrer. Die anderen müssen erraten, woran er denkt.

a) Is it a thing?	No, ______________
b) Is it an animal?	No, ______________
c) Is it in this room?	No, ______________
d) Have you got it at home?	No, ______________
e) Is it a person?	Yes, ______________
f) Is it a man?	Yes, ______________
g) Is it a teacher?	Yes, ______________
h) Is he a terrible teacher?	No, ______________
i) Has he got an old dirty car?	Yes, ______________
j) Is it our English teacher?	Yes, ______________

3

Stelle einige Fragen an Jenny und gib ihre Antworten.

– why she isn't at Tom's party	(ill)
– if she is really ill	(yes)
– what she has got	(a cold)
– if she is unhappy that she can't come	(yes)
– if she has got a present for Tom	(yes)
– if it is a football	(no)
– what it is then	(a secret)

7 Das *present progressive*

Die Verlaufsform des Präsens, das *present progressive*, wird mit den Formen von *to be* und einer *ing*-Form gebildet. Das *present progressive* besteht daher immer aus zwei Teilen.

Es wird vor allem für Handlungen verwendet, die zur Zeit des Sprechens nicht vorbei sind, sondern noch andauern.

Bei verneinten Formen steht *not* oder die entsprechende Kurzform.

Die *ing*-Form *(present participle)* wird mit dem Infinitiv des Verbs + der Endung *-ing* gebildet.

What **are** they **doing**?

Tom's father	**is**	**cleaning**	his car.
Timmy	**is not**	**helping**	him.
Tom and Jenny	**are**	**doing**	their homework.
They	**aren't**	**playing**	in the garden.

Beachte bei der Bildung der *ing*-Form:

- com**e** + ing — co**m**ing
  Ein auslautendes -**e**, das nicht gesprochen wird, entfällt.

- si**t** + ing — si**tt**ing
  swi**m** + ing — swi**mm**ing
  Bei einsilbigen Verben mit kurzem, betontem Vokal wird der auslautende Konsonant verdoppelt.

- l**ie** + ing — l**y**ing
  ie wird vor folgendem *-ing* zu **y**.

1 At Tom's party

Auf der Party sind alle mit irgendetwas beschäftigt. Was tun sie gerade?

1. Mike/take/photos.
2. John/sit at the kitchen table/and drink/all the lemonade.
3. Kate/skip.
4. Tom/ring up/Jenny.
5. Betty/flirt/with Kevin.
6. Two boys/play/football in the kitchen.
7. Some girls/dance/in the kitchen.
8. Ann/lie on the floor/and watch/a film on TV.
9. Jim and Barbara/eat/sandwiches.
10. Susan/sit in a corner/and read a magazine.

2 Timmy's report

Timmy ist auch auf der Party, aber er ist noch sehr klein und stört manchmal. Deshalb schickt ihn Tom zu seiner Mutter. Timmy erzählt ihr, was die anderen machen. Stimmt das, was Timmy sagt? Kannst du ihn korrigieren?

Beispiel: That's not right, Timmy. Mike isn't playing with his camera, he's taking photos.

1. Mike is playing with his camera.
2. John is eating all the sandwiches.
3. Kate is hopping around like a rabbit.
4. Tom is talking to his teacher.
5. Betty and Kevin are kissing.
6. Two boys are quarrelling about a ball.
7. Some girls are running around in the kitchen.
8. Ann is lying on the floor because she is ill.
9. Jim and Barabara are making sandwiches.
10. Susan is reading my picture book.

Wie verwende ich das *present progressive* in Fragen?

- Bei Fragen im *present progressive* steht zunächst eine Form von **to be**, dann das Subjekt und schließlich das *present participle*.
- Fragewörter wie *why, where, when, what* werden einfach vor die Form von **to be** gesetzt. Die Wortstellung ändert sich dadurch nicht.

  Are you talk**ing** to your teacher, Tom?
  Is Jenny ly**ing** in bed?
  Why is she ly**ing** in bed?
  What are her parents do**ing**?

- Bei Kurzantworten wird das *present participle* ausgelassen:

  Is Jenny lying in bed? Yes, **she is**. (Pronomen + bejahte Langform)
  No, **she isn't**. (Pronomen + verneinte Kurzform)

3 Timmy's answers

Timmys Mutter kann nicht ganz glauben, was Timmy ihr erzählt. Daher stellt sie ihm ein paar Fragen. Stelle erst diese Fragen und gib dann Timmys Antworten.

Beispiel: Is Tom really talking to his teacher? Yes, he is.
Is John really eating all the sandwiches? …

4 Timmy is on the way again …

Timmys Mutter glaubt immer noch, dass Timmy manches nicht richtig begriffen hat. Sie schickt ihn daher mit einigen Fragen zurück, damit er nachfragt. Stelle du Timmys Fragen und lasse dir die Antworten geben.

Beispiel: What are you doing, Kate? – I'm skipping.

Timmy's mother wants to know

- what Kate is doing,
- if Tom is really talking to his teacher,
- what Mike is doing with his camera,
- if Susan is really reading his picture book,
- why Ann is lying on the floor,
- if Kate is playing a new game,
- what the boys are doing in the kitchen,
- what the girls are doing in the kitchen,
- if John is still hungry.

5 In Timmy's room

Lies dir den Text der drei Szenen durch und frage dann nach den unterstrichenen Ausdrücken. Verwende dabei die richtigen Fragewörter: *who* ? (wer?) – *where* ? (wo, wohin?) – *what* ? (was?) – *when* ? (wann?)

First scene:

At 7.30 the party is over. The children are going home. They are all happy. Timmy is happy, too. He is in his room. He is lying on the floor, but he isn't crying. He's playing with Tom's birthday presents. They are in his room now. One parcel is open. There's a picture book and some chocolate in it.

Second scene:

Timmy is still lying on the floor. There is chocolate on his face and hands. He isn't playing any more. He's got a pencil in his hand and he is drawing a picture in Tom's picture book. What is Timmy drawing? He's drawing farm animals – red hens, blue dogs and green cows.

Third scene:

Somebody is coming upstairs. He is shouting a name. It is Timmy's brother. He is looking for his presents. He is angry. He is opening the door of Timmy's room. But the room is empty. Where is Timmy? Can you see him?

1

Was machen die Schüler gerade? Stelle Fragen nach den unterstrichenen Wörtern.

Betty/do/her homework.
Mark/make/a paper plane.
Tony and Tom/fight with each other.
Jimmy/lie/on the floor/and/cry.
Kate/clean the board.
Pete and John/play/a game.
Jim/have/his second breakfast.
Mike/run/around in the classroom.

2

Nicht bei allen Lehrern ist Ruhe, wenn sie ins Klassenzimmer kommen. So auch hier. Ergänze bitte.

Teacher: Hey, Bob? What ____________________? **(do)**
__________ still ____________________ with Sue? **(flirt)**

Bob: No, sir, __________ just ____________________ her a question. **(ask)**

Teacher: And what about you, Betty? ____________________ still
______________ your homework? **(do)**

Betty: I __________ not ______________ my homework, sir.
I ____________________ notes. **(do, take)**

Teacher: John, why ________________ still ______________? **(eat)**
You will get fat if you go on like this.

Teacher: And you Jimmy, why ________________ still ______________? **(cry)**
Look at the girls, they ____________________________ at you.
(laugh)

Teacher: And Sam, can you stop singing now? ______________ you all
____________________ now? **(listen)** Then we may start.

8 Modale Hilfsverben

8.1 Die Formen der modalen Hilfsverben

Modale Hilfsverben kennst du auch aus dem Deutschen.
Es entsprechen dabei:

can	können, dürfen
can't/cannot	nicht können, nicht dürfen
must	müssen
mustn't	nicht dürfen
needn't	nicht müssen, nicht brauchen

Beachte: Die verneinte Form von **must** ist **needn't**!

Für „dürfen" bzw. „nicht dürfen" kann in Fragen und Kurzantworten auch **may** (statt *can*) bzw. **may not** (statt *mustn't, can't*) stehen:

May I help you? Yes, you **may**. – No, you **may not**.

Englische Hilfsverben weisen folgende Eigenschaften auf:

1. Sie haben keinen Infinitiv und kein -*s* in der 3. Person Singular.
2. Ihre Formen sind für alle Personen gleich.
3. Hilfsverben können im Englischen nicht alleine stehen; ihnen muss immer ein Verb folgen (eine Ausnahme bilden die Kurzantworten).

   Vergleiche: Er **kann** Englisch. He **can speak** English.
4. Wie im Deutschen folgt einem Hilfsverb immer ein Infinitiv.
5. Objekte und andere Ergänzungen stehen im Englischen immer nach der Verbgruppe.

   Vergleiche: Er kann **sie** sehen. He can see **her.**

1 After the party

Unterstreiche im folgenden Text die modalen Hilfsverben.

After the party Kate can go to her room. It isn't her birthday, so she needn't help. But Tom must. He must help his mother wash up the dishes and clean the kitchen floor. Then they must tidy up the living room. Must Timmy help, too? No, he needn't. He must go to bed because it's already late. He is very unhappy. "Why can't I help you? Why must I always go to bed?" he cries. "Look, Timmy," his mother says, "it's already 8 o'clock; you must go to bed now. You can stay up longer next year." But Timmy is still unhappy. "I can wash the dishes, too." "OK, Timmy, you can help Tom with the dishes, but you mustn't drop them," his mother says. "Fetch the dirty plates from the living room," Tom says to him. Timmy is happy now. He is big and strong and he can help. But what's that? There is a loud noise in the living room, then everything is quiet again. When Tom opens the door, Timmy is gone, but there are three plates on the floor …

2 Right or wrong?

Lies den Text in Aufgabe 1 noch einmal und verbessere, was falsch ist.

1. Kate must go to her room.
2. She mustn't help Tom.
3. Tom must clean Kate's room.
4. He needn't wash up the dishes.
5. He must clean the kitchen floor.
6. He must clean the kitchen windows, too.
7. Timmy can help him.
8. Timmy must clean the kitchen floor, too.
9. Timmy must drop the plates.
10. Timmy can stay up a little longer.

3 A phone call

Am nächsten Tag ruft Tom Jenny an. Jennys Mutter ist am Telefon. Ergänze die modalen Hilfsverben.

Tom:	*Jenny's mother:*
________ I talk to Jenny, please?	Sorry, Tom, you ____________ . Jenny's in the bathroom.
________ Jenny come tomorrow?	No, she ____________ get up.
________ she stay in bed all day?	Yes, she ________.
________ she take medicine?	No, she ______________.
________ I see her this afternoon?	No, you ____________ see her today.
________ I see her tomorrow?	Well, let's see what the doctor says. But you ________ ring her up again in the evening.

4 What Jenny must do

Endlich ist Jenny am Telefon. Sie erzählt Tom, was sie tun muss oder nicht tun darf. Kannst du aufschreiben, was sie sagt?

Beginne so: I *must/mustn't* ...

5 Jenny is really ill

Was kann, darf, muss, braucht Jenny nicht zu tun? Bilde Sätze.

take her medicine **watch TV** **ride on her bike** **read a book**

clean her room **go to school** **help her mother in the kitchen**

do her homework **listen to music** **ring up her friends**

play football **kiss her doctor** **write letters** **wash her clothes**

8.2 Der Gebrauch modaler Hilfsverben in Fragen und Kurzantworten

Bei Fragen steht das Hilfsverb vor dem Subjekt; nach dem Subjekt steht immer der Infinitiv.

Bei Kurzantworten wird nur das Hilfsverb wiederholt, für das Subjekt steht ein Pronomen.

Hilfsverb	**+ Subjekt**	**+ Infinitiv**	
Can	**Kate**	**get** up?	Yes, she can. No, she **can't.**
Must	**she**	**stay** in bed?	Yes, she **must.** No, she **needn't.**

Zu den modalen Hilfsverben, die häufig in Fragen verwendet werden, gehört auch **shall**. Mit **Shall I/Shall we** … ? kann man einen Wunsch erfragen oder ein Angebot machen. Dies ist allerdings nur mit **I** und **we** möglich.

Shall	**+ Subjekt**	**+ Infinitiv**	
Shall	**I**	**open**	the window for you? Soll ich … ?
Shall	**I**	**give**	you your medicine? Soll ich … ?
Shall	**we**	**call**	the doctor again? Sollen wir … ?

6 At the doctor's

Wenn du krank bist, wirst du deinem Arzt gewiss ein paar Fragen stellen. Kannst du seine Antworten geben?

1.	Must I go to school?	No, ______________________.
2.	Must I stay in bed?	Yes, ______________________.
3.	Must I do my homework?	No, ______________________.
4.	Must I stay in bed all day?	Yes, ______________________.
5.	Can I get up?	No, ______________________.
6.	Can I ring up my friends?	Yes, ______________________.
7.	Must I take my temperature?	Yes, ______________________.
8.	May my friends come to see me	Yes, ______________________, but not on the first day.
9.	Can I watch TV?	Yes, ______________________.
10.	Must I take all that medicine?	Yes, ______________________.

7 Your questions

Dein Freund oder deine Freundin ist krank. Du besuchst ihn/sie. Bilde die entsprechenden Fragen und gib die Kurzantworten.

– if he/she is very ill	(Yes)
– if he/she must stay in bed	(Yes)
– if he/she must stay indoors all day	(Yes)
– if he/she may get up for an hour or two	(Yes)
– if he/she has got a temperature	(Yes)
– if he/she can go to school on Thursday	(No)
– if he/she is happy that she needn't go to school	(Yes)
– if his/her teachers are happy, too	(No)

8 Timmy

Vervollständige die Sätze.

1. Timmy is three. He ________________ go to school. (Er braucht nicht . . .)
2. He _________ go to kindergarten. (Er kann . . .)
3. He _________ play with other children there. (Er kann . . .)
4. _________ he go there every day? (Muss er . . . ?)
5. No, he ________________. (Nein, er muss nicht.)
6. _________ he go there alone? (Darf er . . . ?)
7. No, he ________________. (Nein, er darf nicht.)
8. _________ he take his bike? No, he ________________. (Darf er . . . ? Nein, er darf nicht.) It's too dangerous.
9. _________ Tom fetch him in the afternoon? (Muss Tom . . .)
10. Yes, he _________ on Thursdays and Fridays. (Ja, er muss . . .)

9 Helping people

Deine Mutter ist krank. Was kannst du für sie tun? Hier sind ein paar Ideen. Bilde Fragen mit "Shall I …"?

Beispiel: Shall I do the shopping for you?

do the washing up · *do the shopping* · *make your bed*
clean the rooms · *buy you some lemonade* · *go to the chemist's*
get your medicine · *open the window* · *ring up the doctor*
cook the meals · *look after my sister/brother* · *make an appointment*

1

Bilde Sätze. Gib auf die Wortstellung Acht.

a) A doctor must/his patients/examine.
b) Their temperature/must/he/take.
c) Listen/he/must/what they tell him/to.
d) A prescription/give/them/must/he.
e) Go and see/must/he/his patients.
f) Ask/them/how they feel/must/he.
g) He/his patients/to hospital/must send/when they are seriously ill.

2

Stimmt das, was hier steht? Wenn nicht, korrigiere, was nicht richtig ist.

a) A good patient can do what the doctor tells him/her.
b) A good patient mustn't take his/her medicine.
c) A good patient needn't stay in bed when he/she is ill.
d) A good patient mustn't forget his/her appointment.
e) A good patient mustn't be late at the doctor's surgery.
f) A good patient mustn't listen to his/her doctor.

3

Einige Leute helfen gerne. Gehörst du auch dazu? Was sagst du dann?

Jenny:	I can't understand this exercise.	You: *Shall I explain it to you?*
Kate:	My school bag is so heavy.	You: ______________________
Timmy:	I'm so hungry.	You: ______________________
Tom:	I can't find my English book.	You: ______________________
Mike:	I can't do this exercise.	You: ______________________
Sarah:	My windows are so dirty.	You: ______________________
Kevin:	I' m not very good at German.	You: ______________________
Paul:	It's so cold in here.	You: ______________________
Susan:	It's Ann's birthday tomorrow.	You: ______________________

9 Das *simple present* von Vollverben

9.1 Das *simple present* in bejahten Sätzen

Vollverben sind Verben, die im Gegensatz zu Hilfsverben allein im Satz stehen können. Sie kommen im Englischen wie im Deutschen in verschiedenen Zeiten *(tenses)* vor. Eine dieser Zeiten ist das *simple present*.

Formen

I	**like**	ice cream.
You	**like**	sweets.
My father	**likes**	tennis.
My mother	**likes**	English.
A cat	**likes**	mice.
We	**like**	Tom.
You	**like**	us.
They	**like**	TV.

Bis auf die 3. Person Singular hat das *simple present* die gleiche Form wie der Infinitiv (ohne *to*).
In der 3. Person Singular *(he, she, it)* wird ein -*s* angehängt.

Bei der Schreibung der 3. Person Singular gibt es folgende Besonderheiten:

- Bei Verben, die auf die Laute [s], [ʃ], [tʃ] enden, hängt man ein **-es** [iz] an:

  He always catch**es** the bus at six o'clock.

- Bei Verben, die auf einen **Konsonanten + y** enden, wird das **-ys** zu **-ies**:

  to f**ly** — He fl**ies** to France.

- Bei Verben, die auf einen **Vokal + y** enden, ändert sich das **-y** nicht:

  to st**a**y — He sta**ys** with his friends.

- Auch bei *to go* und *to do* wird in der 3. Person Singular ein -**es** angehängt:

  He go**es** home. He do**es** his homework.

1 What Tom does

Verwende das *simple present*.

1. He ____________ at 7 o'clock every morning (get up).
2. Then he ____________ (wash) and ________ on his clothes (put).
3. Then he ________ down to the dining room (go).
4. There he ________ breakfast (have).
5. Then he ____________ for his school bag (look).
6. After that he ____________ the house (leave).
7. Then he ________ to the bus stop (go).
8. He usually ____________ the bus when it is cold (take).
9. He ______________ at school at a quarter to nine (arrive).
10. He ________ hello to his friends (say).

2 What they usually do after lessons

Bilde die folgenden Sätze.

- Tom/go home/do his homework with Jenny/play games/watch TV

  ____

- Kate/go to her room/listen to music/ring up her friends/play

  ____

- Mike/sit in front of his computer/play computer games/often forget his homework

  ____

- Ann and Barbara/send SMS messages/listen to music/read magazines

  ____

- John/have tea/eat a lot of sandwiches/lie down on his bed/have a nap

  ____

9.2 Das *simple present* in verneinten Sätzen

Bei der Verneinung musst du eine Form von *to do* gebrauchen. Diese Form lautet in der 3. Person Singular *does not* bzw. *doesn't*, in den anderen Personen *do not* bzw. *don't*. Das folgende Verb steht im Infinitiv; d. h. du darfst dann in der 3. Person kein *-s* oder *-es* anhängen.

Formenübersicht

I	**don't**	**like**	maths.
You	**don't**	**like**	biology.
Tom	**doesn't**	**like**	maths.
Jenny	**doesn't**	**like**	English.
We	**don't**	**like**	our teacher.
You	**don't**	**like**	geography.
They	**don't**	**like**	their teacher.

Beachte:
Ist *to do* ein Vollverb, so heißt die Verneinung **don't do/doesn't do**:

He **doesn't do** his homework. They **don't do** their homework.

3 A strange family

Die Browns wohnen ganz in der Nähe. Sie haben vier Kinder.
Was tun sie nicht?

1. They ____________ in the morning. (get up)
2. They ____________ an early breakfast. (have)
3. Mr Brown ____________ his car. (wash)
4. Mrs Brown ________ the cooking. (do)
5. Often, their children ________ school. (go)
6. They ____________ school. (like)
7. Helen ____________ her teachers. (like)
8. She ________ her homework. (do)

4 People are different

Bilde Sätze nach dem folgenden Muster.

Beispiel: Tom likes bananas, but he doesn't like oranges.

Tom		Jenny + Kate		Timmy		Mike		The Browns	
bananas	+	volleyball	+	cornflakes	+	photos	+	work	–
oranges	–	tennis	–	tea	–	comics	–	sleeping	+
Jenny	+	sports	+	dogs	+	music	+	books	–
Ben	–	all sports	–	cats	–	singing	–	TV	+

5 Over to you

Was magst du, was magst du nicht? Was mögen deine Freunde/Freundinnen, deine Eltern? Was mögen sie nicht? Schreibe 10 Sätze auf.

Beispiel: I like football, but my father doesn't. He likes tennis.

9.3 Das *simple present* in Fragen und Kurzantworten

Bei Fragen mit einem Vollverb musst du immer eine Form von *to do* verwenden. Wie bei der Verneinung steht das Verb im Infinitiv.

In der Kurzantwort steht für das Vollverb immer eine Form von *to do*.

Do you **like** football?	Yes, **I do**.
	No, **I don't**.
Does your mother **like** football, too?	Yes, **she does**.
	No, **she doesn't**.

Beachte: Wenn **to do** ein Vollverb ist, muss es auch bei Fragen wiederholt werden.

Do you always **do** your homework?	Yes, I **do**.
Do you often **do** it in the morning?	No, I **don't**.

Die Wortstellung *form of to do + subject + infinitive* bleibt auch dann erhalten, wenn die Frage mit einem Fragewort beginnt.

When	**does**	Mike	**get**	up?
When	**do**	his parents	**get**	up?
What	**do**	they	**do**	then?
Why	**does**	Mike	**get**	up at 7?
How	**does**	his sister	**go**	to school?
When	**do**	his parents	**take**	him there?
What subjects	**doesn't**	he	**like**?	

Beachte: to do muss wiederholt werden, wenn es ein Vollverb ist.

What **does** Mike **do** in the evenings?
What **do** you **do** at school?

6 Mike

Mike ist neu in Toms Klasse. Am ersten Tag stellen ihm seine Klassenkameraden viele Fragen. Stelle die Fragen und gib Mikes Antworten.

1. ______________ you like your new school? (Yes)
2. ______________ you play football? (Yes)
3. ______________ your sister go to our school? (Yes)
4. ______________ she play tennis? (No)
5. ______________ you and your sister go to school by bike? (Yes)
6. ______________ you play an instrument? (No)
7. ______________ your father work in York? (Yes)
8. ______________ your mother like York? (Yes)
9. ______________ your parents like it here? (Yes)

7 An interview

Frage deinen Freund/deine Freundin und gib seine/ihre Antworten.

1. Where/you/live?
2. When/get up/in the morning?
3. When/your mother/get up?
4. What/have/for breakfast?
5. Why/not like/cornflakes?
6. When/your parents/leave the house?
7. When/they/come home again?
8. How/get/to school?
9. Why/not take/the bus?
10. What/do/in the afternoon?
11. What games/do/like?
12. What/do in the evening?
13. When/go/to bed?
14. When/your parents/go to bed?

8 Mike

Frage nach den unterstrichenen Wörtern. Benutze das richtige Fragewort.

Mike lives in York now. He likes his new school, but he doesn't like all his subjects. He goes to school by bike. In winter and when it rains, his mother drives him to school. The first lesson begins at 8.45, so he gets up at 7. He leaves the house at a quarter to eight and usually arrives at school at 8.30. He has lunch at school because his parents don't come home until the evening. After school he often goes to see Tom. They play games together until 6 or 7 o'clock or do their homework. Then Mike goes home.

9 Mike's father

Kannst du ihn interviewen?

1. He gets up at 5.30 o'clock in the morning.

   When ______________________ you ______________________?

2. He starts work at 7 o'clock. When ______________________?

3. He leaves his house at 6.30. When ______________________?

4. He drives a school bus. What ______________________?

5. He collects the children from the villages.

   Who ______________________?

6. He takes them to school. Where ______________________?

7. School starts at a quarter to nine.

   When ______________________?

8. In the afternoon he fetches them from school.

   When ______________________?

9. He takes them home again.

   Where ______________________?

10. Then he cleans the bus.

    What ______________________?

11. He often finds things in the bus.

    What ______________________?

1

Bilde Sätze mit den folgenden Verben. Verwende nur die 3. Person Singular.

Beispiel: to fetch My brother fetches a chair.

to go, to carry, to wear, to write, to lose, to want, to use, to sound, to take, to teach, to throw, to tie, to do, to love, to miss, to see, to brush, to choose, to close, to empty, to fly

2

Füge die richtigen Verben ein.

know listen find do make talk show try have

When the pupils ______________ lessons with Mr Cummins, they all ______________. He ______________ a lot of things to ______________ his lessons interesting. He ______________ to them about foreign countries, and even ______________ them how to use the Internet. Here they often ______________ a lot of information about the subjects they ______________ about. But he can be very funny, too. He ______________ a lot of jokes and when they ______________ a problem, he always ______________ and ______________ to help.

3

Es gibt vielleicht ein Mädchen oder einen Jungen in deiner Klasse, die/den du viel besser kennen möchtest. Also stellst du ihr/ihm die folgenden Fragen …

- when he/she usually gets home
- what he/she usually does after school
- if he/she likes going to the cinema
- what kind of films he/she likes
- if he/she often goes to the cinema
- when he/she does her homework
- how much time he/she needs for it

10 *Simple present* und *present progressive*

Wann verwende ich das *present progressive*?

Das *present progressive* verwendet man für Handlungen, die zur Zeit des Sprechens nicht vorbei sind, sondern noch andauern.

> Look! The boy **is doing** his homework.
> He**'s doing a** German exercise now.

Signalwörter dafür sind zum Beispiel: *now, at this moment, look, listen, today, this morning (afternoon, evening).*

Wann verwende ich das *simple present*?

Das *simple present* gebraucht man für wiederholte, gewohnheitsmäßige und lang andauernde Handlungen:

> He usually **does** his homework after school.
> He **goes** to a comprehensive school.

Signalwörter sind: *always, often, sometimes, never, usually, seldom (= selten), every day (week, month, year), in the morning (afternoon, evening).*

Beachte: *Always, often, usually, never* stehen im *simple present* immer vor dem Verb:

> He **usually** does his homework after school.
> He **often** does it in his room.

Sometimes kann auch am Satzanfang stehen:

> **Sometimes** he forgets it, too.

Das *simple present* steht im Englischen auch für aufeinander folgende Handlungen. Solche Handlungen kommen vor allem in Erzählungen und Berichten vor. **Signalwörter** sind z. B.: *first, then, after that, next, soon, at last*. Schau dir dazu diesen Text an:

After school Mike often goes to see Tom. **When** they arrive at Tom's, they **first** put their school bags in a corner. **Then** they go to Tom's room. There they play for an hour or two. **After that** they do their homework together. **Then** Mike goes home.

1 Mike's photos

Mike fotografiert gern. Hier sind ein paar seiner Fotos. Kannst du den Text vervollständigen?

This is Dad.
sit/bus

This is Dad again.
clean/bus

This is our house.
live/there

This is Mum.
leave the house/
always leave at 8

This is our garden .
Look! Mum/work in it/
like her garden

This is our corner shop.
Mum/work there/
sell something

2 Things are different today

Setze das *simple present* oder *present progressive* ein.

1. Mike usually ______________ up at 7, but today he is still in bed. (get) He ______________. (still sleep)
2. He usually ______________ breakfast at 7.30, but today he ______________ in bed. (have; still lie)
3. He often ______________ no time to wash, but this morning he ______________ a bath. (have; take)
4. He usually ______________ his school uniform, but today he ______________ different clothes (put on; wear)
5. He usually ______________ lunch at school, but today he ______________ lunch at home. (have)
6. Mike usually ______________ his mother with the dishes, but today he needn't. His father ______________ the dishes. (help; wash)
7. His parents usually ______________ the house in the morning, but things are different today. They ______________ for a walk. (leave; go)

   Do you know why? Well, it's ______________.

3 What about your Sundays?

Was tust du oft, nie, selten, manchmal usw. am Sonntag? Hier sind ein paar Ideen:

On Sundays I	always never usually sometimes often seldom	get up late play football watch TV play computer games clean my room help Mum and Dad listen to CDs brush my shoes learn English go for a walk write letters go to Church

4 Mr Mason

Toms Vater ist Tierarzt. So sieht ein normaler Arbeitstag bei ihm aus:

7.00	get up at seven o'clock
7.00 – 7.30	wash
7.30	have breakfast
8.00	get in his car
8.30	open his surgery
9.00 – 12.00	examine sick animals
12.30	have lunch at a restaurant
17.00	have a cup of tea
17.30	close the door of the surgery
18.00	come home

Schreibe auf, was Toms Vater jeden Tag tut. Verwende dabei Signalwörter wie *first, then, after that*.

5 What you do

Schreibe auf, was du jeden Tag machst. Verwende dabei alle Signalwörter, die du kennst.

6 Scrambled eggs

Heute sind Toms Eltern nicht zu Hause. Die Kinder haben Hunger. Sie sehen im Kühlschrank nach, aber außer ein paar Eier ist nichts drin. Also machen sie Rühreier. Bilde Sätze und bringe sie in die richtige Reihenfolge.

add some milk, salt and pepper *eat them* *put the eggs in a bowl*

put the scrambled eggs on a plate *stir the eggs*

put everything in the frying pan *break the eggs*

cook the eggs in the frying pan *put fat in the frying pan*

7 Another breakfast

Simple present oder *present progressive*? Setze die richtigen Formen ein.

1. The weather is fine and the sun ________________ (shine). It is already ten o'clock, and the Masons ______ still ____________ (sit) at the breakfast table.
2. It's Sunday. The Masons always ____________ (have) a late breakfast on Sundays. But somebody ______ still ____________ (miss). It's Kate. She is still in her room; she ________________ (sleep).
3. So Timmy ____________ (go) to Kate's room. He ____________ (open) the door and ________________ (see) that Kate is still in her bed. He ______________ (try) to wake her up, but Kate ________________ (not listen), so Timmy ______________ (go) back and ______________ (tell) his dad that Kate ______ still asleep.
4. Mr Mason ______________ (say): "Come on, Timmy. Get Tom's water pistol and ask your sister if she ________________ (not want) to get up now."
5. So Timmy ________________ (fetch) Tom's water pistol and ____________________ (go) to Kate's room. Suddenly there is a loud noise and somebody ____________________ (shout) in an angry voice: "You just wait, Timmy. When I get you, I..."

1

Simple present oder *present progressive*? Vervollständige die Sätze.

a) Mike ____________________ a photo of his new school.
He ____________________ taking photos. (take; like)

b) He ____________________ only ____________________ photos of schools, he ____________________ photos of everything. (not take; take)

c) He always ____________________ his photos on a CD.
Look! He is ____________________ in a new CD now. (put)

d) He ____________________ them in his desk. (keep)

e) Sometimes he ____________________ them to his friends. (show)

2

Fülle die Lücken mit den angegebenen Verben aus.

Anne ____________________ (like) music. She ____________________ (learn) to play the piano. Anne's baby sister Jane ____________________ (like) the piano, too, because she can make a lot of noise on it. One night when everybody is already in bed, Anne ____________________ (wake) up. What is it? She ____________________ (sit) up in her bed and ____________________ (listen). It's the piano. Somebody ____________________ (play) it. Who can that be? Oh, Jane of course! Anne ____________________ (jump) out of bed, ____________________ (rush) downstairs and ____________________ (switch) on the lights. But there is nobody there. "Jane, come here! I know that you are there!" There is no answer. Anne ____________________ (turn) off the lights and ____________________ (go) upstairs to Jane's room. Jane is in her bed and she ____________________ (sleep). Anne ____________________ (hear) the piano again …

11 Verneinung, Fragen und Kurzantworten

11.1 Die Verneinung

Tom schreibt manchmal in der Schule Briefe an seine Freundin Jenny. Hier ist einer davon, aber jemand hat den Brief gefunden und Tom einen Streich gespielt. Der Brief ist nämlich verändert:

> Dear Jenny, I hope we can't see each other this afternoon. I haven't got a lot of homework to do, but I don't think I can come at 4 o'clock. Can you wait for me at the bus stop? I hope I can't come. I really don't want to see you again. You aren't the nicest girl I know. I am not always thinking of you.
>
> You don't know that I don't like you.
>
> Love, (ha! ha!) Tom

Wenn du den Brief anschaust, siehst du, dass die Verneinung im Englischen nur bei den Vollverben im *simple present* mit einer Form von *to do* – mit **do not/does not** bzw. **don't/doesn't** – gebildet wird.

Bei den Formen von *to be, have got,* den Hilfsverben *can, may* usw. und dem *present progressive* wird die Verneinung nur mit *not* gebildet.

Beispiele:

Jenny **isn't** the nicest girl.	**to be**
He **isn't thinking** of her.	**present progressive**
He **can't** see her. **auxiliary**	
He **hasn't got** a lot of homework.	**have got**

Vergleiche aber:

He **doesn't like** her.	**simple present**

1 What is right?

Was denkst du, dass Jenny tut, wenn sie den Brief erhält? Bilde die folgenden Sätze.

Beispiel: I think Jenny doesn't begin to cry.

1. She begins to cry.
2. She is very unhappy.
3. She must leave the classroom.
4. She must laugh.
5. She writes a letter, too.
6. She shows it to her teacher.
7. She reads it to the class.
8. She goes home immediately.
9. She falls ill.
10. She kicks Tom.
11. She is very angry with him.
12. All her neighbours begin to laugh.

2 Good pupils

Was sind gute Schüler für dich? Hier sind ein paar Ideen. Verwende auch verneinte Formen.

1. Good pupils are silly.
2. Good pupils work too much.
3. Good pupils are bad at sports.
4. Good pupils always do their homework.
5. Good pupils never forget anything.
6. Good pupils never make their teachers angry.
7. Good pupils never talk in lessons.
8. Good pupils have got a lot of friends.
9. Good pupils always talk to their teachers.
10. Good pupils are unhappy.
11. Good pupils are only interested in school.
12. Good pupils never go out with boys/girls.
13. Good pupils always talk about school.
14. Good pupils know everything.
15. Good pupils never play computer games.

11.2 Die Fragebildung

Auch Fragen werden im *simple present* mit **to do** gebildet. Wie bei der Verneinung steht das entsprechende Vollverb dann im Infinitiv:

Does	Tom	**like**	Jenny?
Do	Tom's parents	**like**	her, too?

Bei den Formen von *to be, have got* und den Hilfsverben wie *can, must* darfst du **to do** nicht verwenden. Dies gilt auch für das *present progressive*.

Is	Tom		happy?
Has	he	**got**	a girlfriend?
Is	he	**writing**	her a letter?
Can	he	**see**	her?

3 An article for the school magazine

Tom schreibt einen Artikel über Schüler, die sich an der Schule nicht wohl fühlen. Er möchte eine Art Fragekatalog aufstellen, um die Gründe dafür herauszufinden. Kannst du seine Fragen formulieren?

Beispiel: Are you often alone?

Tom wants to know if

- they are often alone,
- they like their parents,
- they have got any friends,
- they have got any hobbies,
- their parents often play with them,
- they have got anybody to talk to,
- they watch a lot of TV,
- most of their teachers are nice,
- they are often afraid when they are alone,
- their parents are often out in the evening.

4 Pupils, pupils ...

Wie du weißt, sind nicht alle Schüler gleich. Frage deinen Nachbar/deine Nachbarin und versuche herauszufinden, was für ein Schüler/eine Schülerin er/sie ist.

- There are pupils who
- can't sit still,
- talk all the time,
- can't listen,
- listen only when the teacher gets angry, – often forget things,
- don't do their homework,
- find everything boring, – often sleep during lessons,
- are often late,
- are often ill for tests,
- only like sports.

5 You and your school

Bilde Fragen.

1. _______ you _______________ school? **(like)**
2. _______ you often _______________ your homework? **(forget)**
3. _______ you _______________ your homework now? **(do – present progr.)**
4. _______ your mum _______________ you now? **(help – present progr.)**
5. _________ your parents often _______________ you? **(help)**
6. _________ you _______________ nice teachers? **(have got)**
7. _________ they _______________ you? **(like)**
8. _________ they _______________ you a lot of homework? **(give)**
9. _________ you _______________ during lessons? **(can talk)**
10. _________ you _______________ chewing gum in the English lessons? **(may eat)**
11. _________ you _______________ a school magazine at your school? **(have got)**
12. _________ you _______________ it? **(read)**
13. _________ you _______________ it interesting? **(find)**

11.3 Entscheidungsfragen und Kurzantworten

Bei Fragen musst du zwischen zwei Grundtypen unterscheiden, nämlich zwischen Entscheidungsfragen und Ergänzungsfragen.

Bei Entscheidungsfragen will man wissen, ob sich eine Sache so oder so verhält. Man antwortet daher immer mit Ja oder Nein. Im Englischen entspricht diesem Ja oder Nein eine Kurzantwort. Vergleiche:

to be	**Is** Kate ill?	Yes, **she is**. No, **she isn't**.
present progressive	**Is** she **sleeping**?	Yes, **she is**. No, **she isn't**.
auxiliary	**Must** she **see** a doctor?	Yes, **she must**. No, **she needn't**.
have got	**Has** she **got** a cold?	Yes, **she has**. No, **she hasn't**.
simple present	**Does** she **go** to school?	Yes, **she does**. No, **she doesn't**.
	Do her friends **look** after her?	Yes, **they do**. No, **they don't**.

Beachte:

- Für Vollverben im *simple present* tritt eine Form von **to do** ein.
- Das Subjekt der Kurzantwort ist immer ein Pronomen (*I*, *you* usw.).
- Nach *yes* steht eine Langform, nach *no* die Kurzform.
- Ist **this** oder **that** das Subjekt des Fragesatzes, so steht in der Kurzantwort immer **it**.

  Is **this** your brother? Yes, **it** is.
  Is **that** your mother? Yes, **it** is.

6 Timmy's new picture book

Während Tom in seinem Zimmer schreibt, kommt Timmy herein. Er hat sein neues Bilderbuch dabei und den Kopf voller Fragen. Kannst du sie beantworten? Gib Kurzantworten bitte.

1. Look at that house, Tom. Is that a church?
2. The man with the hat – is that a postman?
3. And what is he doing? Is he trying to get into the house?
4. And what about those men? Are they climbing the ladder?
5. Or are they running away?
6. Is the man running after the two other men?
7. Does he want to catch them?
8. Are they afraid of him?
9. Is he a policeman?
10. Do they want to steal the bike?
11. Do they want to ride away on it?
12. Is that a bike, too?

11.4 Ergänzungsfragen

Im Unterschied zu Entscheidungsfragen will man bei Ergänzungsfragen eine zusätzliche Information über eine Sache oder eine Person. Sie beginnen daher immer mit einem Fragewort. Kurzantworten mit *yes* oder *no* sind nach Ergänzungsfragen nicht möglich.

Bei Ergänzungsfragen musst du beachten, ob du nach dem Subjekt eines Satzes oder nach anderen Satzteilen fragen willst.

Fragen nach dem Subjekt

Bei der Frage nach dem Subjekt nimmt das Fragewort die Stelle des Subjekts ein. Das Verb steht – wie im Deutschen – immer in der 3. Person Singular. Die Umschreibung mit **to do** wird nur in verneinten Fragen verwendet.

Who	has got	a new pet?	**Jenny** has.
Who	must look	after it?	**Jenny** must.
Who	is looking	after it?	**Jenny** is.
Who	buys	its food?	**Jenny** does.
Who	doesn't pay	for its food?	**Jenny** doesn't.
Whose dad	pays	for it?	**Jenny's dad** does.

Fragen nach dem Objekt

Bei Fragen mit den Formen von **to be** und **have got** oder mit den Hilfsverben **can, must** usw. wird keine Form von **to do** gebraucht. **To do** steht nur bei Vollverben im *simple present*.

Where	are	you?	
What	are	you	doing?
Who	are	you	ringing up?
What	has	she	got?
What	must	she	do?
Where	must	she	go?
What	does	she	say?
Who	does	she	help?
Where	does	she	go?

Beachte:
Mit ***who*** (wer/wen) und ***what*** (was) kannst du sowohl nach dem Subjekt als auch nach dem Objekt fragen:

Who likes Tom?	**What** happens?
Who does Tom like?	**What** does she do?

what	(was)	fragt nach Sachen
who	(wer/wen)	fragt nach Personen
whose	(wessen)	fragt nach dem Besitzer
why	(warum)	fragt nach dem Grund
where	(wo/wohin)	fragt nach dem Ort oder der Richtung
when	(wann)	fragt nach der Zeit
how	(wie)	fragt nach dem Wie

7 Some questions for you

Schau dir noch mal Timmys Bilderbuch an. Trage das richtige Fragewort ein. Manchmal sind auch zwei verschiedene Fragewörter möglich.

1. ______________ building can you see in this picture?
2. ______________ high are the walls?
3. ______________ is behind the walls?
4. ______________ are these people there?
5. ______________ is leaning against one wall?
6. ______________ many people can you see?
7. ______________ are they doing?
8. ______________ is running away?
9. ______________ are they running away?
10. ______________ are the two men?
11. ______________ is the bike?
12. ______________ is running after them?
13. ______________ is the man trying to do?

8 Your questions

Frage nach dem Subjekt der folgenden Sätze.

1. Timmy doesn't know the building in his picture book.
2. Its walls are very high.
3. A ladder is leaning against the wall.
4. Two people are running away.
5. They are running to a bike.
6. A policeman is running after them.
7. He wants to catch them.
8. He hasn't got a uniform on.
9. The two men are afraid of him.

9 Jenny

Frage nach den unterstrichenen Wörtern oder Ausdrücken.

1. <u>Jenny</u> is Tom's girlfriend.
2. <u>Her parents</u> are from Leeds.
3. They have got <u>a car</u>.
4. Sometimes <u>her parents</u> are strict (= streng).
5. <u>She</u> can't always see <u>Tom</u>.
6. She must tell <u>her parents</u> <u>where she is going</u>.
7. <u>She</u> must be back <u>early</u>.
8. She mustn't be out after 8 o'clock <u>in the evening</u>.
9. Listen! <u>The telephone</u> is ringing.
10. <u>Tom</u> is <u>at home</u>.
11. Jenny is ringing up <u>Tom</u>.
12. <u>She's</u> very <u>excited</u>.

10 A phone call

Jenny möchte Tom etwas sagen, aber die Verbindung ist sehr schlecht. Daher muss Tom dauernd fragen, was sie gesagt hat.

Beispiel: *Jenny:* "I've got a new pet." *Tom:* "What have you got?"

Jenny:	*Tom:*
"I have got a new pet."	"What ______________________?"
"A new pet. It's a hamster."	"What ______________________?"
"I like it."	"What ______________________?"
"I must buy some food for it."	"What ______________________?"
"Food. Can you come to the pet shop?"	"Where must ________________?"
"Can you lend me some money?"	"What must _________________?"
"I want to buy a book about hamsters, too."	"What ______________________?"
"A book about hamsters. I don't know anything about hamsters."	"I can't understand you. The line is very bad."
"____________________________?"	"The line. I can't understand you."
"____________________________?"	"You. Let's meet at the pet shop then."
"At the pet shop? Yes, OK, at three o'clock."	"OK. See you then."

11 Bingo

Jenny und Tom treffen sich in der Tierhandlung. Sie kaufen ein Buch und Futter für Jennys Hamster. Dann gehen sie im Park spazieren. Dort sehen sie zwei Mädchen und einen Mann mit einem Hund. Die Mädchen stellen dem Mann viele Fragen über seinen Hund. Hier sind seine Antworten. Wie lauteten die Fragen?

1. How old ______________________? He's nearly two years old.
2. Where ______________________? He sleeps in the hall.
3. When ______________________? I usually get up at six.
4. What ______________________? Then I make him his breakfast.
5. What ______________________? Usually, he has some dog food.
6. When ______________________? Well, I take him for a walk after breakfast.
7. When ______________________? I go to work at half past eight.
8. Where ______________________? I take him to my neighbour's house.
9. How long ______________________? He stays there until I come home.
10. Where ______________________? We play in the garden.
11. What ______________________? I try to teach him some tricks.
12. What ______________________? In the evening? Well, we watch TV together.
13. What films ______________________? He likes westerns.
14. Why ______________________? Well, he likes horses.
15. What ______________________? He always barks when he sees them.
16. Why ______________________ now? Look! There is a girl over there. She is riding a horse.

1

Verneine die folgenden Sätze.

Beispiel: Jenny hasn't got a cat, she has got a hamster.

a) Jenny has got a cat. **(a hamster)**
b) She keeps it in her bedroom. **(a cage downstairs)**
c) It sleeps in her bed. **(its cage)**
d) Jenny must talk to it a lot. **(it's not a budgie)**
e) Tom must catch mice for it. **(it's not a cat)**
f) She takes it to school. **(teachers not like that)**

2

Gib Kurzantworten.

a) Have you got a cat? ______________________
b) Do you like cats? ______________________
c) Has any of your friends got a cat? ______________________
d) Do they like pets? ______________________
e) Must you buy food for your pet? Yes, you ______________________
f) Must you keep it in a cage? No, ______________________
g) Must your pet sleep in your bed? No, ______________________

3

Stelle Fragen mit *who, whose, what* und *where.*

a) Jenny has got a boyfriend. **(who/what)**
b) His photo is on the wall. **(whose/where)**
c) He likes her. **(who/who)**
d) She likes him. **(who/who)**
e) Her parents like him, too. **(who/who)**
f) They are in the same class. **(who/where)**
g) They often go home together. **(who/where)**
h) Tom often rings her up. **(who/who)**
i) Sometimes they are happy. **(who/what)**

12 Zeitformen zur Wiedergabe der Zukunft

12.1 Das *will*-Futur

Im Deutschen gebrauchen wir für zukünftige Handlungen meist nicht das Futur, sondern das Präsens. Im Englischen muss dagegen fast immer ein Futur stehen, wenn eine Handlung in der Zukunft stattfindet.

Formen

Das *will*-Futur *(will-future)* wird mit *will* + Infinitiv (bei Kurzformen: *'ll* + Infinitiv) gebildet. Verneinte Formen bildet man mit *will not* (Kurzform: *won't*) + Infinitiv, Fragen durch Umstellung von Subjekt und Prädikat. Bei Kurzantworten steht nur *will* oder *won't*.

Eine Form von **to do** ist bei **will** nicht möglich.

What **will happen** next year?	Kate **will be** twelve.
When **will** she **be** twelve?	She**'ll be** twelve in May.
Will she **be** happy then?	Yes, she **will**.
Will she **be** unhappy?	No, she **won't**.

Gebrauch

Das *will*-Futur wird verwendet

- für neutrale zukünftige Handlungen oder Ereignisse und Vorhersagen:

  Kate **will be** twelve in May.
  All her friends **will come**.

- für Vermutungen und um eine Hoffnung auszudrücken. Dies ist besonders nach *perhaps* und Verben wie *I think, I believe, I'm sure, I hope* der Fall:

  I **hope** the weather **will be** nice.
  Perhaps she**'ll have** a big party, too.
  I think I**'ll go**.

- bei spontanen Entschlüssen:

  "I must buy a present for her." "Oh, then I'**ll buy** her a present, too."

- im Hauptsatz von Nebensätzen der Bedingung:

  If you go to her party, I'**ll go**, too.
  But I'**ll go** only if she invites me.

- im Hauptsatz von Nebensätzen der Zeit:

  When I see her, I'**ll ask** her.
  I'**ll tell** you when we see each other again.

1 An excursion

Kates Klasse macht einen Ausflug ans Meer. Vervollständige bitte, was ihr Englischlehrer sagt, bevor sie losfahren.

1. I think/the weather be nice
2. I don't think/it rain again
3. I hope/we spend a nice day together there
4. I hope/water not too cold
5. If the water isn't too cold/we go for a swim
6. I hope/you have a good time

2 What will happen if …

Bilde Sätze.

Beispiel: If the coach is late, they won't leave at 8 o'clock.

What will happen	if the coach is late? if it rains all day? if the sun doesn't shine? if some of the children are late? if their teacher is ill? if there is too much traffic?

3 Questions

a) Die Schüler haben viele Fragen. Schreibe sie auf.

b) Stelle dir vor, du wärst der Englischlehrer. Was würdest du antworten?

Jenny:
when we be there?
we need a warm pullover?
you buy us an ice cream?

Peter:
what games we play?
we be allowed to walk around on our own?

Kevin:
lunch on the beach?
play games on the beach?
our maths teacher come with us?

Susan:
have time enough to go shopping?
when back? go back bus/train?

4 Kate's hopes

Kate freut sich auf diesen Ausflug. Sie hofft, dass …

not rain

lots of fun

interesting things to see

weather/nice

her friends go, too

enough pocket money

no homework for the next day

not ill

not too many teachers

not get a cold

a) Bilde Sätze mit *she hopes, thinks, she's sure, perhaps* usw.

b) Was würdest du von einem solchen Ausflug erwarten?

Beginne so: *I hope …*

5 On the beach

Was tun die Schüler, wenn sie am Strand sind? Bilde Sätze mit den folgenden Angaben.

When they are on the beach,	take off their clothes play games go for a swim look for shells* splash* their teacher with water have a picnic be very noisy run around rush into the water

*shell – Muschel
*to splash – bespritzen

6 There are nice people

Bevor sie ans Meer gehen, machen sie eine Stadtbesichtigung. Vervollständige bitte, was sie dabei sagen.

Kate: My bag is very heavy. There are too many things in it.

Ben: *I'll carry it for you.*

Christine: I must buy something to drink.

Catherine: I'll buy you somethig to drink.

Jane: Look at these postcards. I need some.

Helen: I'll can buy them for you.

Susan: Look at that girl. I'll talk to her.

Jim: No problem. ____________________.

Kevin: I'm so hungry. I think I'll have a sandwich.

Ronny: Well, then ____________________.

12.2 Das *going to*-Futur

Formen

Das *going to*-Futur *(going to-future)* wird mit dem Präsens von *to be + going to* gebildet. Dem *to* folgt ein Infinitiv. Verneinte Formen werden mit *not* gebildet, Fragen durch Umstellung von Subjekt und Prädikat.

"What **are** you **going to** do on your birthday, Kate?"
"I**'m going to** have a party and I**'m going to** invite all my friends."
"**Are you going to** invite Ben, too?" Yes, I am."
"And what about Ronny? **Are you going to** invite him, too?"
"No, I'm not. **I'm not going to** invite him."

Achtung:
Verwechsle das *going to*-Futur nicht mit dem *present progressive*:

present progressive	**going to-Futur**
He**'s going** home.	He**'s going to** go home.
(Er geht gerade nach Hause.)	(Er hat vor, nach Hause zu gehen.)

Gebrauch

Wenn du ausdrücken willst, dass jemand etwas in der Zukunft plant oder tun will, musst du das *going to*-Futur verwenden. Dies gilt vor allem dann, wenn diese Absicht schon länger bestand.

7 Plans, plans, plans ...

Alle haben sich etwas vorgenommen. Trage bitte die richtigen Verben ein.

write help buy do spend go invite clean work

1. Kate's tests aren't very good, so she *is going to work* harder.
2. Jenny thinks that Kate's tests aren't very nice. So she is going to help her.
3. Kate doesn't like Ben. So she isn't going to invite him.
4. Helen likes Ben. She is going to write him this afternoon.

5. Linda's bike is very old. Her parents are going to buy her a new bike.
6. Betty's room is very dirty. What is she going to do? Well, she is going to clean it.
7. Mary is looking forward to the holidays. She is going to go to the seaside.
8. She is going to spend her holidays there.

8 Asking the others about their plans

Schau dir die Aufgabe 7 noch einmal an. Frage bitte Kate, Jenny und die anderen nach dem, was sie vorhaben.

Beispiel: What are you going to do about your tests?
Are you going to work harder?

9 The *will-* or *going to*-future?

Kate hat bald Geburtstag. Dazu gehen ihr einige Gedanken durch den Kopf.

1. If the weather is fine, we will play in the garden.
2. I think everybody will like that.
3. But I hope Ben will not come (not).
I 'm not going to invite him (not).
4. There are still so many things to do. Perhaps Jenny will help me.
5. Where is my shopping list? I hope Tom will help me with the lemonade. I 'm going to ask him when I see him.
6. And who is going to buy all the rest?
7. What can I do with Timmy? Well, I will ask Mum if she can take him for a long, long walk.
Perhaps he will be tired when he gets back.

10 Planning a test

Dein Lehrer hat euch gesagt, dass ihr nächsten Montag eine Klassenarbeit schreiben werdet. Verwende das *going to-* oder das *will*-Futur in den folgenden Sätzen.

1. "Well, there's no need to hurry. We ____________ write it before next Monday. There's plenty of time to prepare it. I think I ____________ start next Sunday."
2. "Why bother? I ____________ ask my father if he has the time to help me. He's always happy when he gets good marks."
3. "A test next Monday? What ____________ it ____________ be about, by the way? I think I ____________ have to ask John about it."
4. "All right, all right, I don't think it ____________ be very difficult. And I've got a good neighbour. We are a good team. And I'm quite sure he ____________ help me this time, too."
5. "I'm always a bit nervous before tests, so I always take my time to prepare them. If I don't start to prepare it today, I ____________ be terribly nervous on Monday."
6. "A test? Okay, but why on Monday? Doesn't he know that there is an important football match next weekend? I ____________ (not) miss it. And if I don't find the time to prepare the test, well, then I ____________ (not go) to school."

1

Hilfst du gern anderen Leuten? Dann sage ihnen, was du tun willst.

a) "I don't like my English homework." *"Then I'll do it for you."*

b) "My room is so dirty." ____________________

c) "My school bag is so heavy." ____________________

d) "I haven't got any money." ____________________

e) "Where's my pen? I can't find it." ____________________

f) "Where are my shoes?
Are they in my room?" ____________________

g) "I don't want to kiss my girlfriend." *"Oh,* __________________ *"*

2

Übersetze die folgenden Sätze. Achte auf die Zeiten, die du verwendest!

a) Morgen schreiben wir einen Englisch-Test.
b) Ich hoffe, er ist nicht zu schwer.
c) Ich hoffe, meine Nachbarin hilft mir.
d) Vielleicht bekomme ich dann eine gute Note.
e) Ich frage sie heute Abend, ob sie mir helfen will.
f) Wenn sie mir hilft, gebe ich ihr eine Tafel Schokolade.
g) Ich gebe sie ihr aber nur, wenn ich eine gute Note habe.
h) Wenn ich keine gute Note habe, esse ich die Schokolade selbst *(= myself)*.

3

Was willst du am nächsten Wochenende machen? Schreibe auf, was du tun und was du nicht tun willst.

help Mum · *go to school* · *play computer games* · *play football*
play with my teddy · *get up late* · *go for a walk*
go and see my friends · *go mountain climbing* · *go to the beach*
tidy up my room · *clean my bike* · *work for school*
go for a walk with my friend · *see my teacher* · *eat a lot of ice cream*
play with my parents

13 Das *present perfect*

13.1 Die Formen des *present perfect*

Formen

Das *present perfect* wird mit dem Präsens von *have* (in der 3. Person Singular *has*) und dem *past participle* (Partizip der Vergangenheit) gebildet. Die Kurzformen von *have ('ve/'s)* sind natürlich auch möglich.

Verneinte Formen bildest du mit *not*, Fragen durch die Umstellung von Subjekt und *has/have*. Wie bei allen zusammengesetzten Zeiten sind Formen von *to do* bei der Frage und Verneinung nicht möglich.

Die regelmäßige Form des *past participle* wird durch Anhängen der Endung -**ed** an den Infinitiv gebildet:

to finish	he has finish**ed**
to talk	she has talk**ed**
to play	they have play**ed**

Besonderheiten bei der Bildung des *past participle*

- Ein auslautendes -**e**, das nicht gesprochen wird, entfällt:

  to arrive he has arriv**ed**

- Bei einsilbigen Verben mit kurzem, betonten Vokal wird der auslautende Konsonant verdoppelt:

  to stop he has sto**pped**

- Nach Konsonant wird -**y** zu -**i**:

  to cry he has cr**ied**

Beachte:
Neben den regelmäßigen Formen des *past participle* gibt es im Englischen genau wie im Deutschen auch unregelmäßige Formen. Diese musst du auswendig lernen. Die unregelmäßigen Verben findest du in deinem Lehrbuch und in jedem guten Wörterbuch.

1 The past participle

Bilde die Partizipien der Vergangenheit mit den folgenden Verben.

to live	*lived*	to give	
to carry		to play	
to say		to lie	
to show		to feel	
to catch		to think	
to bring		to tell	
to leave		to buy	
to spend		to stand	
to write		to take	
to keep		to find	
to speak		to know	
to read		to make	
to hear		to begin	

2 The infinitive

Wie lautet der Infinitiv der folgenden Verben?

paid		taught	
chosen		fallen	
lost		dropped	
thrown		tried	
fed		bought	
slept		met	
worn		run	

3 Holiday plans

Dieses Jahr wollen die Masons mit ihrem Wohnwagen zum Lake District fahren. Notiere anhand der Liste in Sätzen, was sie bereits erledigt haben.

- book a place for July
- write to the local tourist office
- have a look at the road map
- try to find out the best route
- begin to check their caravan
- buy a new bottle of gas
- check the tyres
- repair the rear window

4 Preparations

Die Masons richten ihren Wohnwagen für die Reise zum Lake District her. Sie haben sich eine Liste der Dinge gemacht, die noch zu tun sind. Schreibe auf, was sie bereits getan und was sie noch nicht getan haben.

Beispiel: We have washed the caravan, but we haven't cleaned the floor yet.

- wash the caravan ✔
- clean the floor
- clean the windows ✔
- make the beds
- put in some food ✔
- buy a new frying pan
- put in Timmy's toys ✔
- buy a new picture book
- take Tom's tennis racket ✔
- buy new tennis balls
- tell the neighbours to look after the flowers ✔
- give them a key

5 Timmy's questions

Timmy ist sehr aufgeregt. Er möchte wissen, was mit seinen Sachen passiert ist. Stelle Timmys Fragen.

Beispiel: Have you seen my potty?

- buy a new picture book for me
- put it in the caravan
- pack my swimming things
- take away my pencils
- find my red toy car
- put my telephone in the caravan
- see my teddy
- buy some chocolate

Merke
Für die Kurzantworten im *present perfect* gelten die üblichen Regeln: Das Subjekt wird durch ein Pronomen wiederholt; bei bejahten Kurzantworten steht die Langform des Hilfsverbs; bei verneinten Kurzantworten steht die Kurzform des Hilfsverbs.

6 A last check

Bevor sie abfahren, fragt Herr Mason noch einmal alle:

1. "Let me see ... Have we shut all the windows?"

   Mrs Mason: Yes, we have.

2. "Have you been to the neighbours, Jane?"

   Mrs Mason: Yes, ________________________.

3. "Have you locked the back door, Kate?"

   Kate: No, ________________________.

4. "Have you all been to the toilet?"

   All: Yes, ________________________.

5. "Have you lost your teddy again, Timmy?"

   Timmy: No, ________________________.

6. "Have we forgotten anything?"

   All: No, ________________________.

7. "Can we go now?"

   Timmy: No, we ________________________.

   I've left my teddy upstairs.

13.2 Die Wortstellung beim *present perfect*

Wie bei anderen zusammengesetzten Zeiten steht das Objekt im Englischen immer hinter der Verbgruppe und nicht – wie im Deutschen – vor dem Verb.

Vergleiche:

I	have	**done**	**my homework**.
Ich	habe	**meine Hausaufgaben**	**gemacht.**

Von den **Signalwörtern**, die häufig mit dem *present perfect* gebraucht werden, stehen:

- unmittelbar vor dem Verb:
  never (niemals), **ever** (jemals) und **already** (schon)
- am Satzende: **yet** (schon), **not . . . yet** (noch nicht)

  Have you **already** packed your things?
  I have**n't** packed my clothes **yet.**
  Have you **ever** been late?
  Have you finished **yet**?
  I have **never** been late

7 Questions and answers

Stelle die folgenden Fragen und beantworte sie.

Beispiel:
Have you ever driven a caravan? No, I haven't. I've never driven a caravan.
Or: No, I haven't driven a caravan yet.

Have Has	you your father your sister your friends	ever already never	be clean go have drive sleep play	to a caravan site? a caravan? to England? on a caravan holiday? an accident? a caravan? in a caravan? lunch in a caravan?

8 Let's put it right

Hier stimmt etwas mit der Wortstellung nicht. Korrigiere die Sätze.

1. Everything/the Masons/packed have/already.
2. They/to their neighbours/the key of their house/given/have/they.
3. They/in the caravan/all their things/have put.
4. York/have/they left/today.
5. They/already/done/100 kilometres/have.
6. But they/not arrived/have/yet/at their camping site.
7. All/they/enjoyed/have/so far*/their trip.
8. They are sure/never/had/they/such a nice trip/had.
9. Not/yet/been/Timmy/sick*/has.
10. He is hungry. He/yet/not/has/for lunch/anything/had.
11. But he/already/been/on his potty/four times/has.

*so far – bisher

*to be sick – sich übergeben

13.3 Der Gebrauch des *present perfect*

Das *present perfect* benutzt man für Handlungen, die zwar vorbei sind, die aber ein Ergebnis haben, das in der Gegenwart noch wirksam oder sichtbar ist:

"We **have washed** the caravan. It's clean now."
"Where are my car keys? I hope I **haven't lost** them."
"**Have** you **seen** them? Do you know where they are?"

9 What has happened?

Kannst du die folgenden Sätze ausschreiben?

Beispiel: There's lipstick on Tom's face. Jenny has kissed him goodbye.

There's lipstickon Tom's face.
(Jenny – kiss him goodbye)

Here are Mr Mason's car keys.
(find again)

Here are the Masons in front of their caravan. They are ready to leave now.
(pack everything)

Look at that window. It's not shut.
(somebody forget to shut it)

1

Was hast du heute schon gemacht? Bilde Sätze und benutze das *present perfect*.

Beispiel: I have done my homework.

I/wake up
I/get out of bed
I/not wash
I/have breakfast
I/take my dog for a walk
I/hurry to school
I/not be late
I/try to listen
I/not make much noise
I/come here

2

Mike ist heute sehr traurig. Daher stellen ihm seine Freunde viele Fragen.

Beispiel: What has happened, Mike? Have …

what happen
have an accident
you lose your money
write a bad test
see your English teacher
get up on the wrong side of the bed
your girlfriend leave you
not have breakfast
Sandra try to kiss you

3

Bilde Sätze im *present perfect* und korrigiere die Wortstellung.

a) Mike/never/a good worker/be.

b) Never/he/working/like.

c) Two left hands/he/have/always.

d) He/his room/nearly never/clean himself.

e) He/already/his room/clean/today?

14 Das *simple past*

14.1 Die Formen des *simple past*

Wie im Deutschen gibt es auch im Englischen regelmäßige und unregelmäßige Formen des *simple past*. Die unregelmäßigen Verben *(irregular verbs)* musst du dir gut einprägen; eine Liste von ihnen findest du in jedem guten Wörterbuch.

Die Formen des *simple past* sind für alle Personen gleich. Dies gilt sowohl für die regelmäßigen wie die unregelmäßigen Verben.

Bei den regelmäßigen Formen wird das *simple past* wie das *past participle* mit dem Infinitiv + -**ed** gebildet. Dabei gelten für die Schreibung folgende Regeln:

- Bei regelmäßigen Verben, die auf -**e** enden, entfällt das -e.
- Bei regelmäßigen Verben, die mit Konsonant + **y** enden, verändert sich das **y** zu **i**.
- Bei regelmäßigen Verben, die auf einen Konsonanten nach einem kurz gesprochenen Vokal enden, verdoppelt sich der Konsonant.

to live	liv**ed**	to tr**y**	tr**ied**	to sto**p**	sto**pp**ed

Beachte:
Die Formen des *simple past* von *to be* sind unregelmäßig. Sie lauten:

I	**was**	we	**were**
you	**were**	you	**were**
he, she, it	**was**	they	**were**

1 Back at school

Die Kinder sind aus den Ferien zurück und erzählen sich, was sie erlebt haben. Unterstreiche im folgenden Text die regelmäßigen und die unregelmäßigen Formen des *simple past* mit verschiedenen Farben.

Mike:
We visited the Isle of Wight and did quite a lot of things there. I even tried to talk to some Germans there, but they just laughed when I tried to say something in German to them. I think my German sounded a bit funny to them. So I stopped speaking German to them and laughed at their English.

Tom:
We went to the Lake District. We found a fantastic camping site and had a great time there. Only Timmy wasn't very lucky. One day he … but I' ll tell you about that later.

2 Mind the spelling and the pronunciation

Welche dieser Verben sind regelmäßig, welche nicht? Unterstreiche die unregelmäßigen Verben.

say stop lead read
buy write
play sit feel
cry catch set ride
hear
carry swim
think feed
leave
fall meet
fly let break
bring lose get
teach pay

3 Regular and irregular verbs

Setze die folgenden Verben in das *simple past*.

say	said	lead	
play	played	sit	sat
carry	/	lose	
fly	/	write	wrote
buy	/	set	
catch	catched	feed	fed
fall	✓	meet	met
stop	stopped	read	red
leave	leaved	feel	fel
think	thorught	ride	rode
let		make	made
teach	teached	hear	
pay		break	

4 Going on holidays

Vor den Ferien müssen du und deine Eltern viele Dinge erledigen.

You must

- check your car
- put a good map in it
- pack your things
- lock the doors
- shut the windows
- switch off all lights
- say goodbye to your neighbours
- look up the route you want to take

Das hat die Familie Mason bereits alles erledigt. Schreibe auf, was sie getan haben. Verwende das *simple past*.

Beispiel: Before they left, they checked their car, they …

5 The Masons are leaving

Trage die fehlenden Verben ein. Verwende das *simple past*.

know want arrive be leave carry see

come see go run hear get shut

The Masons ___ to leave early, but as usually it ___ quite late when they ___ off. Kate ___ still tired and Tom ___ to finish a letter. Then Timmy's potty ___ missing and nobody ___ where it ___ When they ___ all in the car again, somebody ___ that a window ___ still open. So Mr Mason ___ out of the car, ___ into the house again and ___ it.When he ___ back,Timmy ___ to go to the toilet again.So Mr Mason ___ out of the car again and ___ Timmy to the bathroom. When they ___ back, they ___ the telephone ringing. So Tom ___ out of the car and ___ into the house again. But he ___ not fast enough. When he ___, the line ___ dead. But finally they ___ all in the car and ready to leave.

6 The Masons' trip

Erzähle, was auf der Fahrt zum Campingplatz alles geschah.
Verwende das *simple past*.

finally leave at 10 o'clock
first stop at 11.30
Timmy sick*
lunch at 1 p.m.
forget Timmy's teddy
get into car at 2 p.m.

arrive at 6 p.m. at the camping site
try to put up tent* for Tom
tent collapse
had supper at 8
go to bed at 9
all very tired

*to be sick – sich übergeben
*tent – Zelt

14.2 Das *simple past* in verneinten Sätzen, Entscheidungsfragen und Kurzantworten

Verneinung

Vollverben werden im *simple past* mit *did not* bzw. der Kurzform *didn't* verneint. Danach steht immer der Infinitiv. *Was/were* werden mit *not* verneint. Statt *was not/were not* sind auch die entsprechenden Kurzformen *(wasn't/weren't)* möglich.

Subjekt	**did not**	**(didn't)**	**+ Infinitiv**
Timmy	**did not**	**(didn't)**	**enjoy** the trip.
He	**did not**	**(didn't)**	**feel** fine.
Timmy	**was not**	**(wasn't)**	happy.
Tom and Kate	**were not**	**(weren't)**	sick.

Fragen und Kurzantworten

Das gilt auch für Fragen und Kurzantworten. Wenn du eine Frage im *simple past* mit Vollverben bilden willst, musst du *did* bzw. *didn't* gebrauchen. Danach steht immer ein Infinitiv. In Kurzantworten wird das Vollverb durch *did* bzw. *didn't* ersetzt.

Did	you **have** a nice holiday?	Yes, I **did**.
Didn't	you **go** swimming?	No, I **didn't**.

to be

Bei *to be* ist keine Form von *to do* möglich. Du bildest die Frage allein durch Umstellung von Subjekt und Prädikat. Bei Kurzantworten stehen die entsprechenden Formen von *to be*.

Were	you	on the beach?	No, I **wasn't**.
Was	the water	cold?	Yes, it **was**.
Weren't	you	unhappy?	No, I **wasn't**.

7 The first night

Setze die folgenden Sätze ins *simple past*. Verwende die verneinten Formen.

The first night Timmy not sleep very well – not have his teddy – not quiet enough at the camping site – at home not sleep in the same bed with Kate – his sister not leave him enough room – she not want him in "her" bed – Timmy not warm enough – not have nice dreams – not happy that night.

8 The next morning

Am nächsten Morgen fragt Timmys Mutter, wie seine erste Nacht im Wohnwagen gewesen ist. Stelle ihre Fragen und antworte für Timmy. (Schau dir dazu Aufgabe 7 an).

1. ~~How~~ did ______ you sleep well tonight, Timmy?
2. Did ______ you miss your teddy?
3. Did ______ it quiet enough? / Was
4. Did ______ you sleep with all that noise?
5. ~~How~~ Did ______ Kate leave you enough room?
6. Did ______ you warm enough? / Were
7. Did ______ you have nice dreams?
8. Did ______ you like your first night here?

9 What the Masons did the first day

Formuliere die folgenden Sätze.

Beispiel: The first day they didn't get up early. They had a late breakfast.

	not cook in the caravan	write a letter to Jenny
Timmy	not sick any more	have a late breakfast
Tom	not do any work	go for a walk
Kate	not get up early	buy a new teddy for Timmy
Mr Mason	not do any homework	have lunch in a restaurant
Mrs Mason	not lie on the beach	look for new friends
	not stay in the caravan	feel better

14.3 Das *simple past* in Ergänzungsfragen

Auch bei Ergänzungsfragen, d. h. Fragen mit Fragewörtern, musst du *did* oder *didn't* gebrauchen. Bei Fragen nach dem Subjekt ist *didn't* dagegen nur in verneinten Fragen möglich.

Fragen nach dem Subjekt

Who was on the beach?
What happened?
Who didn't come back?
Who broke his arm?

Fragen nach allen anderen Satzteilen

Where was Timmy?
What did he **do** there?
Why didn't he **come** back?
What did he **break**?

Beachte:
Bei Fragen mit ***to be*** steht **nie** ein ***did***!

10 Tom's letter

Lies den folgenden Bief. Schreibe auf, was die Eltern Kate wohl gefragt haben.

Dear Mike,
Something terrible happened yesterday. I wanted to go to the beach with Timmy and Kate. Timmy had his teddy and his picture book in his hands, so perhaps he didn't see where he was going. Anyway – suddenly Timmy cried and fell over a big stone. I turned round and saw Timmy. He was lying on the ground. He still had his teddy in his hand; but his arm looked strange. Timmy didn't cry at first, but his face looked very white. I didn't know what to do, so I told Kate to run home and to fetch Mum or Dad. Kate did what I told her and five minutes later Mum and Dad were there. They carried Timmy back to the caravan and phoned a doctor. When she came, she examined Timmy …

11 What Mike's parents wanted to know

Als Mike Toms Brief bekam, erzählte er seinen Eltern von Timmys Unfall. Sie wollten viel wissen. Stelle du ihre Fragen.

- why Timmy didn't see the stone
- where the accident happened
- if Timmy broke his arm
- if Timmy cried a lot
- how he looked
- if he was sick
- if they called a doctor
- when the doctor came
- what she told them
- if Timmy had to go to hospital

12 At the hospital

Timmy musste ins Krankenhaus. Dort untersuchte ihn ein Arzt, der ihm einige Fragen stellte. Was fragte er? Was antwortete Timmy?

Beispiel: Did it hurt, Timmy? Yes, it did.

– hurt?	– fall on your arm?	– his teddy all right?
– how?	– cry?	– who help you?
– why?	– when?	– anybody with you?

14.4 Die Vergangenheitsform einiger Hilfsverben

Von den englischen Hilfsverben hat nur *can* (können) eine Vergangenheitsform: *could/could not* bzw. die Kurzform *couldn't*. Für die anderen Hilfsverben musst du Ersatzverben *(substitutes)* verwenden.

Hilfsverb		**Ersatzverb**
may	(dürfen)	**was/were allowed to**
may not/mustn't	(nicht dürfen)	**wasn't/weren't allowed to**
must	(müssen)	**had to**
needn't	(nicht müssen)	**didn't have to**

Beachte:
Nach Hilfsverben und Ersatzverben steht immer ein Infinitiv. Bei Hilfsverben steht jedoch – im Unterschied zu Ersatzverben – kein **to** vor dem Infinitiv!

13 At the hospital

Füge die Vergangenheitsformen der Hilfsverben ein.

1. When the doctor examined Timmy, he found out that Timmy's arm was broken. So Timmy ____________________ go home. **(konnte nicht)**
2. He ____________________ stay in hospital for some days. **(musste)**
3. He ____________________ stay in bed all the time. **(musste nicht)**
4. His parents ____________________ to visit him. **(durften)**
5. His parents ____________________ take him home. **(konnten nicht)**
6. He ____________________ to get up the first day. **(durfte nicht)**
7. But he ____________________ to get up the next day. **(durfte)**

14 Timmy's "jobs"

Die ersten Tage im Krankenhaus durfte Timmy bestimmte Dinge nicht tun. Was konnte, durfte er tun, was nicht? Was musste er tun? Was nicht?

make his bed	– look at his picture book
play with his teddy	– be careful with his arm
draw pictures with his right arm	– talk to the nurses
cook his meals	– run around in the room
clean the room	– stand on his right arm
stay in bed all day	– eat his meals
play in the corridor	– keep his arm still (= ruhig)

15 Questions

Frage Timmy, was er tun musste und was nicht, und gib seine Antworten.

Beispiel: Did you have to stay in bed all the time? – No, I didn't.

16 Prescriptions

Setze die fehlenden Ersatzverben ein.

After three days the Masons ________________ to take Timmy home. They ________________ leave the camping site and break off their holidays, the doctors told them, but there were some things that Timmy ________________ to do. He ________________ to stay in the caravan all day, but he ________________ to be very careful with his arm; he ________________ to play any wild games and above all, he ________________ to swim. He ________________ to take his medicine, and they ________________ to worry, but they ________________ to look after Timmy.

17 When I was ill ...

Du bist doch sicher schon einmal krank gewesen? Was konntest du, durftest du, musstest du tun und was nicht? Schreibe acht Sätze dazu.

Beginne so: *The last time I was ill, I ...*

18 Questions

Als Tom aus den Ferien zurück war, fragten ihn seine Freunde viel. Stelle du ihre Fragen und verwende dabei das *simple past.*

- if he had to go there with his parents
- if they stayed at a hotel
- if he had to sleep in a tent
- if he had to take his German books with him
- if he was allowed to stay up late
- when he had to go to bed
- if he had to help his parents
- what he had to do
- if he made any friends there
- if there were other girls
- why he didn't kiss them
- if they were nicer than Jenny
- what the weather was like
- if he was happy that he was back.

1

Setze Timmys Bericht über seine erste Nacht im Wohnwagen ins *simple past*.

a) I (not sleep) very well.
b) My sister always (take) my blanket away.
c) She always (kick) me.
d) I (be) very tired, but I (can't) sleep.
e) And it (be) very cold.
f) Some people (be) very loud outside.
g) They (shout) and (play) games.
h) I (miss) my teddy.
i) And I (have) a bad dream.
j) It (be) about my teddy.

2

Wie du noch weißt, träumte Timmy schlecht. Hier ist sein Traum. Erzähle du ihn, aber verwende das *simple past*.

Beispiel: My teddy was all alone in the house.

His teddy is all alone in the house. Everybody is gone. He feels very lonely and there are big tears in his eyes. Why have they all left him? And why under the bed? It's dark and dusty there and he can't see a thing. And there are noises in the room, noises he doesn't know. And they come nearer and nearer. He feels that there is somebody or something watching him. What is it? Suddenly he sees two green eyes and feels something touching him, something that is cold and slimy. He tries to run away, but something keeps him back …

3

Es passierten aber auch viele schöne Dinge in den Ferien. Frage nach den unterstrichenen Wörtern. Verwende das *simple past*.

They went <u>to the beach</u> and enjoyed <u>the sea and the sun</u>. <u>They</u> played a lot of games or found the time to read a book or two. Timmy read <u>his new picture book</u>, too. <u>When the weather was fine</u>, they went for long walks <u>in the countryside</u>. They watched <u>the fishermen</u> and their boats. One day, Mr Mason and Tom <u>went fishing</u>, too, and came back with a big fish. "<u>We caught it this morning</u>," they told everybody, but nobody really believed them.

15 *Simple past* oder *past progressive?*

15.1 Der Gebrauch des *simple past*

Das *simple past* steht

- bei Handlungen, die in der Vergangenheit stattfanden und abgeschlossen sind. Es findet sich daher nach **Signalwörtern** wie *yesterday, a (week, a month, year) ago, last Friday (month usw.), in + Jahreszahl*. Oft steht es auch nach *when*:

  Mr Mason **had** an accident, too.
  But this **was** *many years ago*.
  When **did** he **have** the accident?
  It **was** *in 1975, when he was much younger* than today.

- nach wiederholten und gewohnheitsmäßigen Handlungen, die in der Vergangenheit stattfanden. **Signalwörter** sind hier – wie schon beim *simple present* – *always, usually, often, sometimes* usw.:

  He **played** in a football team *then*.
  They **played** *every Saturday*.
  His team **wasn't** a good team, so they *often* **lost**.
  But *sometimes* they also **won**.

- für abgeschlossene, aufeinander folgende Handlungen der Vergangenheit. **Signalwörter** sind hier *first, then, after that, the next moment, the next morning, last night, when, suddenly* usw.:

  One day they **were** on their way home, when their bus *suddenly* **ran off** the road. He **felt** a pain in his left leg, and things **went** black before his eyes. *Then* he **didn't feel** anything else. *Afterwards*, they **told** him that his left leg **was** broken.

1 After the accident

Erzähle Timmys Geschichte. Verbinde die Sätze mit *first, then, after that, so, when* usw.

1. Tom send Kate back to parents
2. Kate run to caravan/Kate tell parents all about Timmy's accident
3. Mrs Mason phone a doctor
4. doctor arrive/examine Timmy/call an ambulance
5. ambulance arrive/the ambulance men put Timmy on a stretcher*/carry him inside the ambulance/drive him to the hospital

*stretcher – Bahre

2 Timmy at the hospital

Im Krankenhaus fragt eine Krankenschwester Timmy, wie es zu dem Armbruch gekommen ist. Erzähle, wie es dazu kam. Verwende das *simple past*.

Tom and Kate – want to go – to the beach – I ask Mum – if I can go there, too. First not want, but then say yes. So I tell Tom to wait for me – I go into the caravan – fetch my teddy – They walk very fast – so I must run – a big stone in my way – not see it – fall over it – break my arm – not let go my teddy – hold it in my hand – I feel pain in my leg – then Tom and Kate come – but I not know what happen then …

15.2 Der Gebrauch des *past progressive*

Das *past progressive* wird mit *was/were* und der *-ing*-Form, dem *present participle*, gebildet.

Bei Fragen wird umgestellt: Hilfsverb – Subjekt – Verb. Verneinte Formen werden mit *not* gebildet. Die Umschreibung mit *to do* ist bei Fragen und bei der Verneinung nicht möglich.

Wann benutze ich das *past progressive*?

Im Unterschied zum *simple past* musst du das *past progressive* für Handlungen verwenden, die zu dem Zeitpunkt noch nicht vorüber waren, als eine neue Handlung einsetzte. Handlungen im *past progressive* bilden den Hintergrund für neu einsetzende Handlungen.

What **were** the Masons **doing** when Timmy had his accident?
Were they **going** to the beach, too? No, they **weren't**.
Mr Mason **was talking** to a neighbour.
They **were having** a coke and **talking** about football.
Mrs Mason **was reading** a book.
She **wasn't listening** to what they **were talking** about.

Signalwörter für die Verwendung des *past progressive* sind **still** und **while**.

3 Bad talk

Ein Nachbar der Familie Mason erzählte allen Leute schlechte Dinge. Bilde ganze Sätze.

When poor Timmy broke his arm,	his parents his mother his father nobody	just get up not look after Timmy lie in the sun smoke and talk still lie in bed write a letter just have breakfast

4 What people were doing

Schau dir das Bild an und schreibe auf, was die Leute gerade taten, als Timmy sich den Arm brach. Beginne so: When Timmy had his accident, …

a woman reading a magazine
a man lying in a deckchair
some people swimming
two children playing with a ball
a boy listening to the radio
a girl putting on her clothes
a family having a picnic

15.3 *Simple past* und *past progressive* im Vergleich

Wie du bereits weißt, steht das *simple past* für Handlungen, die vorüber sind und aufeinander folgen. Solche Handlungsketten kommen vor allem in Erzählungen und Berichten vor. Deshalb musst du das *simple past* in einer Geschichte oder einem Bericht für jede neu einsetzende Handlung verwenden.

Wann benutze ich das *simple past* und wann das *past progressive*?

Um das zu entscheiden, musst du dich fragen:

1. Welche Handlung ist neu? *(simple past)*
2. Was passierte gerade zu dieser Zeit? *(past progressive)*
3. Welche Handlung setzt neu ein? *(simple past)*
4. Was war zu dieser Zeit noch nicht vorbei? *(past progressive)*

Beispiele:

When the ambulance **arrived**, Timmy **was** still **lying** on the beach.
He **was crying**.
The ambulance men **examined** Timmy, while a lot of people **were standing** around them.
Then the ambulance men **put Timmy** on a stretcher and **drove** him off to hospital.
When the ambulance **left**, the people **were** still **standing** there.

Beachte:
Nicht alle Verben können im Englischen eine *progressive form* bilden. Verben wie

to be, to belong, to see, to feel, to hear,
to want, to like, to know, to think, to sound

haben im Englischen meist keine *progressive form*. Hier musst du die *simple forms* gebrauchen.

5 At the doctor's

Nach ein paar Tagen im Krankenhaus durfte Timmy wieder nach Hause. Aber er musste sich beim Hausarzt untersuchen lassen. Im Wartezimmer waren viele Patienten. Warum waren sie hier? Bilde Sätze.

play football/
fall to the ground/
broke my arm

climb a rock/
slip

I slip/have a shower
broke three ribs*

* rib – Rippe

I clean the windows/
ladder break/
fall onto the floor

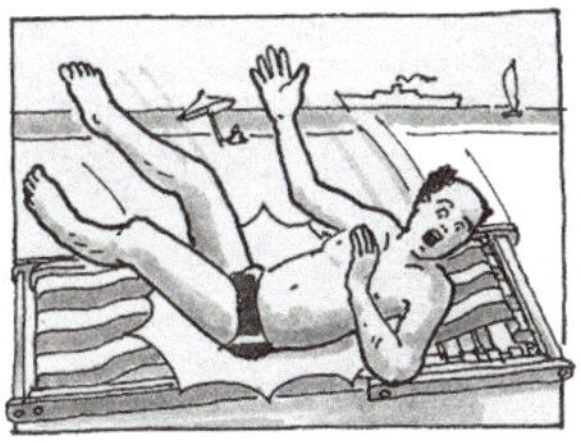

I lie in my deckchair/
it collapse

I do my homework/
fall asleep/
fall off the chair

6 A ghost story

Simple past oder *past progressive*?

Timmy still ______________ (have) to be very careful with his arm and he ______________ (can't) go for a swim, of course. So everybody ______________ (must) to keep him busy. Tom often ________ (read) ghost stories to him. Timmy's favourite story ________ (be) about an American family who ______________ (want) to buy an old castle in England. When they ______________ (come) to the castle, the sun ______________________ (not shine). It __________________ (rain) and thunder ______________ (sound) again and again. When they ______________ (enter) the castle, a flash of lightning* ______________ (fill) the hall and there ________ (be) thunder all through the night. When they ______________ (come) down the next morning, they ______________ (see) some blood* on the floor. The next night they __________________ (hear) strange noises in the corridor outside their bedrooms. When Mr Otis ______________ (open) the door, he ______________ (see) a terrible old man. Long hair ____________ ____________ (fall) from his head, his eyes ______________ (be) like fire and …

7 Timmy's dream

Eines Nachts träumte Timmy schlecht, nachdem ihm Tom eine Gruselgeschichte vorgelesen hatte. Erzähle Timmys Traum. Pass auf die Zeiten auf!

Timmy lie in his bed – his teddy sleep beside him
Suddenly the door open – somebody come into his room
When open his eyes – he see that a dark figure stand in front of his bed/look at him/then sit down on his bed
A cold hand touch his face – he wake up with a loud cry
The lights go on – his mother stand in front of him –
"You dream, Timmy?" she said.

*flash of lightning – Blitz *blood – Blut

1

In dem Augenblick, in dem Timmy sich den Arm brach, geschahen noch andere Dinge. Bilde Sätze.

- the sun shine/not rain
- some people play games
- other people talk to each other
- people eat or have something to drink
- children laugh and shout
- some people swim in the sea
- others lie in the sun
- people put on or take off their clothes
- some people go home.

2

Trage die folgenden Verben ein. Pass auf, ob du das *simple past* oder das *past progressive* verwenden musst.

take lie open unpack put dream sleep

come begin wake wait see carry

a) When Timmy ____________ home, a big suprise ____________ for him.

b) A new picture book ____________ on the table.

c) When Timmy ____________ it, he immediately ____________ it and ____________ to "read".

d) While he ____________, his parents ____________ his things.

e) When they ____________ back, Timmy ____________.

f) Mr Mason ____________ him in his arms and ____________ him upstairs into his room.

g) There he ____________ him in his bed.

h) Timmy ________ not ____________ up; he ____________ of doctors, ghosts and other things.

16 *Simple past* und *present perfect*

16.1 Perfekt im Deutschen und *simple past* im Englischen

Wenn du das *present perfect* und das *simple past* im Englischen verstehen willst, musst du umdenken, da die Verwendung beider Zeiten vom Deutschen stark abweicht.

Verwechsle das *simple past* und *present perfect* nicht mit dem Perfekt im Deutschen!

Vergleiche:

> „Gestern **sind** wir **heimgekommen;** wir **haben** unser Gepäck aus dem Auto **geholt** und **haben** dann zu Abend **gegessen.** Dann **sind** wir ins Bett **gegangen** und **sind sofort eingeschlafen**."
>
> "Yesterday we **came** home; we **fetched** our luggage from the car; then we **had** supper. After that we **went** to bed and **fell** asleep immediately."

In der deutschen Umgangssprache gebraucht man das Perfekt vor allem dazu, eine Geschichte zu erzählen oder über etwas zu berichten, das vorbei ist. Dies ist im Englischen mit dem *present perfect* nicht möglich.

Wenn man im Englischen etwas erzählen oder berichten will, verwendet man das *simple past*. Es ist die eigentliche Erzählzeit im Englischen und findet sich daher auch nach **Signalwörtern** wie *first, then, after that, at that moment, suddenly* usw.

1 The first lesson

Tom und seine Klasse lernen Deutsch. In der ersten Stunde nach den Ferien mussten sie ihrem Deutschlehrer über ihre Ferien berichten. Kannst du übersetzen, was sie sagten?

1. Wir sind gestern zurückgekommen.
2. Ich bin oft schwimmen gegangen.
3. Ich habe Mike in den Ferien getroffen.
4. Ich habe einen deutschen Jungen kennen gelernt.
5. Ich habe sehr viel Deutsch gesprochen.
6. Wir haben einen Unfall gehabt.
7. Ich habe keine Hausaufgaben in den Ferien gemacht.
8. Ich habe in den Ferien zu viel gegessen.
9. Ich bin richtig dick geworden.
10. Wir haben in den Ferien viele Schlösser besichtigt. *(to visit)*

2 Mike's story

In einer der ersten Stunden nach den Ferien mussten Tom und seine Mitschüler einen Aufsatz über ihre Ferienerlebnisse schreiben. Hier sind Mikes Notizen für seinen Aufsatz. Kannst du ihn schreiben? Pass auf die Zeiten auf!

In the holidays we visit Carisbroke Castle – old castle – famous, too, because Charles I prisoner there some hundred years ago before his execution. People say – he not found peace yet – his ghost still walk there.

When we come there, the sky very dark – when walk through the entrance – begin to rain – so go into the castle – very dark in there, too; lots of strange noises – suddenly a door open – when I look there – I see something green – come towards me – run out of the building and tell everything to my parents – not believe me – just laugh at me.

After the holidays over – we must go home again – The first night I go to bed early, but wake up at midnight – strange noise – see something green – it sit at my desk – it write something in an exercise book – I very afraid, not move – five minutes later it gone. I get up – go to the desk – there see my German exercise book – open – a note in the book – it run: DON'T DO ANY HOMEWORK TOMORROW OR YOU'LL DIE! This is what the ghost tell me – that's why I not do any homework last Tuesday.

16.2 Der Gebrauch von *simple past* und *present perfect*

Gebrauch

Das *simple past* steht für Handlungen, die abgeschlossen und daher vorüber sind. (Siehe dazu auch Kapitel 15.)

Das *present perfect* steht für Handlungen, die zwar vorbei sind, aber für die Gegenwart noch Folgen haben. In dieser Funktion steht das *present perfect* immer ohne eine Zeitangabe der Vergangenheit.

Mit dem *present perfect* oft benutzte **Signalwörter** sind:

already (schon), **yet** (schon), **not ... yet** (noch ... nicht), **never** (niemals) und **ever** (jemals).

Vergleiche:

The Masons **have packed** everything.	They **packed** yesterday.
They **have turned** off the gas.	They **turned** the gas off after breakfast.
They **have already locked** the door.	When **did** they **lock** the door?
They **have paid** for the camping site, too.	They **paid** ten weeks ago.

3 Mike's photos

Während der Ferien hat Mike viele Fotos gemacht. Hier zeigt er sie Tom und Jenny. Vervollständige die Sätze. Verwende dabei die richtigen Zeiten *(simple present, simple past, present perfect)*.

Look! This our hotel/ stay there for two weeks

That is the beach in front of our hotel/always go swimming there

This is our car/accident/ we not repair it yet

This is Carisbrooke Castle/ visit the castle/you know that Charles I prisoner here?

That is Tim. I play with him a lot/we often go to the beach/have a swim together

And that girl over there – his sister/we play with her sometimes

4 Back at school

Alle Schüler sind wieder von den Ferien zurück. Sie stellen einander viele Fragen. Stell du diese Fragen. Entscheide dabei, ob du das *simple past* oder das *present perfect* verwenden musst.

1. When ______________ you ______________ come back?
2. Where ______________ you ______________ go?
3. ______________ you ______________ (like) your stay there?
4. ______________ ever ______________ (be) to Italy?
5. ______________ you ______________ (do) anything for school as our teacher ______________ (tell) you?
6. ______________ you ______________ (play) tennis in the holidays?
7. How many postcards ______________ you ______________ (write)?
8. Where ______________ you ______________ (buy) these shoes?
9. What ______________ (be) the weather like? ______________ it ______________ (rain) a lot?
10. ______________ you already ______________ (see) Mike? Is he late again?

5 So sorry, but ...

Nicht alle Schüler mögen Hausaufgaben. Gehörst du auch dazu? Dann findest du hier einige Entschuldigungen, die du deinem Lehrer sagen kannst, wenn du sie nicht gemacht hast. Achte auf die Zeiten!

		my neighbour (be) ill.
		I (not remember) where I (put) it.
		I (leave) my book at school.
		I (leave) it on the bus/at home.
		my mother father/sister (be) ill yesterday.
	B	I (feel) so ill in the afternoon.
	E	my pen (not work).
I couldn't do my homework,	C	I (forget) my school bag.
	A	my baby brother/baby sister (ruin) it.
I can't show you my	U	my computer (break) down.
homework,	S	my printer (not) work.
	E	my exercise book (be) full.
		my baby brother (make) a plane out of it.
		I (must) repair my bike.
		my mother (not have) time to help me.
		somebody (steal) it.
		I (cannot) open my school bag.

1

Übersetze bitte.

a) Ich habe das Gepäck ins Auto getan.
b) Dann sind wir alle eingestiegen.
c) An einer Verkehrsampel mussten wir halten.
d) Da ist uns jemand in unser Auto gefahren *(= crash into).*
e) Wir sind alle ausgestiegen.
f) Verletzt *(= injured)* war niemand.
g) Aber unser Auto war beschädigt *(= damaged).*
h) Dann mussten wir auf die Polizei warten und konnten nicht weiterfahren.

2

Trage die richtigen Zeiten (*simple past* oder *present perfect*) im folgenden Telefongespräch ein.

Tom: Guess who it is? Well, it's me, Tom. ________ you ________ **(get)** my letters? I ________ **(write)** the last one two days ago.

Jenny: Hi, Tom. Nice to hear your voice again. I ________ **(get)** your other letters, but I ________ **(get)** the last one yet. How many ________ you ________ **(write)** ?

Tom: I think about ten. But tell me, when ________ you ________ **(come)** back?

Jenny: I ________ **(come)** back two days ago.

Tom: How ________ you ________ **(like)** London?

Jenny: Well, I ________ **(like)** it, but my aunt ________ **(be)** terrible sometimes. She just ________ **(think)** that I ________ **(be)** a small baby. She always ________ **(say)** that I ________ **(be)** too young to look after myself. And she ________ **(not like)** your letters, Tom.

Tom: But why? ________ she ________ **(not like)** my handwriting?

Jenny: Don't be stupid, Tom. She thinks it's not good for a girl of my age to talk to boys.

17 Adjektive

17.1 Der Gebrauch des Adjektivs

Adjektive beziehen sich immer auf Substantive oder Pronomen. Dabei geben sie Eigenschaften der jeweiligen Sachen oder Personen an.

Wie im Deutschen steht das Adjektiv auch im Englischen immer unmittelbar vor dem Substantiv *(a nice boy)*.

Nach bestimmten Verben wie z. B. *to be* steht es auch nach dem Substantiv: *Tom is nice*.

Are there any **nice** and **clever girls/boys** in your class?
Or are **they** all **silly** and **stupid?**

1 What's your English teacher, friend, brother, sister like?

Wähle drei Adjektive für jede Person, die du beschreibst, von der folgenden Liste aus:

Beispiel: What's your English teacher like? Let me see – he/she is clever and intelligent, but he/she can be strange, too. And what about your …

bad, beautiful, good, boring, busy, careful, crazy, exciting, fantastic, noisy, fat, loud, modern, poor, powerful, quick, slow, strange, tall, small, thin, strong, worried, nice, clever, intelligent, funny, heavy, dangerous, interesting, wonderful, difficult

2 And what about your dream girl/dream boy?

Wie sollte er/sie sein? Was für ein Mädchen/Junge möchtest du als Freund/Freundin haben? Schreibe dazu fünf Sätze. Benutze die Adjektive von Aufgabe 1.

3 Your idea again

Wähle nochmals drei Adjektive von der Liste in Aufgabe 1 aus und schreibe, was du über die folgenden Dinge oder Personen denkst:

Beispiel: Girls are nice, clever and intelligent.

English tests *boys* *comics* *TV* *computers*
books *baby* *brothers/sisters* *books* *teachers*
films *pop music* *football* *TV* *girls*

4 What's the opposite?

Stelle Gegensatzpaare auf.

Beispiel: A good teacher – a bad teacher

a funny girl	____________	a clever pupil	____________
an old town	____________	a quiet boy	____________
a small boy	____________	a happy child	____________
a good mark	____________	a difficult text	____________
a boring film	____________	a silly person	____________
a fast runner	____________	a terrible story	____________
a bad driver	____________	a rich man	____________
a slow worker	____________	a dirty room	____________

17.2 Die Steigerung des Adjektivs

Die Grundform oder Grundstufe, also die ungesteigerte Form eines Adjektivs, heißt Positiv *(positive)*, die 1. Steigerungsstufe Komparativ *(comparative)* und die Höchststufe der Steigerung Superlativ *(superlative)*.

Adjektive werden im Englischen wie folgt gesteigert:

Positiv	**Komparativ**	**Superlativ**
poor	poor**er**	the poor**est**
big	bi**gger**	the bi**ggest**
funn**y**	funn**ier**	the funn**iest**
clev**er**	clever**er**	the clever**est**
famous	**more** famous	the **most** famous
difficult	**more** difficult	the **most** difficult

Für die Steigerung von Adjektiven gelten folgende Regeln:

- Adjektive mit einer Silbe *(poor, fine)* und zweisilbige Adjektive auf -**y** und -**er** *(funny, angry, clever)* bilden den Komparativ mit -**er** und den Superlativ mit -**est**. Dabei entfällt ein auslautendes -**e**.
- Bei Adjektiven, die auf -**y** enden, wird das -**y** zu -**i** (happier, the happiest).
- Einsilbige Adjektive mit einem kurzen, betonten Vokal, die auf Konsonant enden, verdoppeln den auslautenden Konsonanten (bigger, the biggest).
- Zweisilbige Adjektive, die nicht auf -**y** und -**er** enden sowie alle Adjektive, die mehr als zwei Silben haben, bilden den Komparativ mit **more** und den Superlativ mit **most**.

Beachte:
Die folgenden Adjektive haben unregelmäßige Steigerungsformen:

good	**better**	**the best**
bad	**worse**	**the worst**

5 Comparatives and superlatives

Bilde die Komparative und Superlative der Adjektive, die du in Aufgabe 1 findest.

6 Tom's family

Schau dir die Personen an und vergleiche sie. Verwende die Komparative von *tall* und *small*.

17.3 Der Vergleich im Satz

Die verschiedenen Formen der Adjektive benutzt man oft dazu, Vergleiche zu ziehen. Gleichheit bzw. Ungleichheit werden dabei folgendermaßen ausgedrückt:

Gleichheit:

Mike is **as** tall **as** Tom. Is he also **as** intelligent?	**as** + **positive** + **as**

Ungleichheit:

Tom's sister is**n't as** tall **as** Mike.	**not as** + **positive + as**
She is small**er than** Mike.	**comparative** + **than**
But she is **more intelligent than** Mike.	

Beachte:
Vor und nach der Grundform des Adjektivs steht immer **as**, nach dem Komparativ dagegen immer **than**.

Achtung: Verwechsle *than* (als) nicht mit *then* (dann, damals).

7 Comparisons

Susan und Betty, zwei Mädchen aus Toms Klasse, mögen einander nicht besonders. Daher sind sie oft verschiedener Meinung.

Beispiel: *Susan:* I think football is more exciting than volleyball.
Betty: No, it isn't, but it's more dangerous.
Susan: More dangerous? I think volleyball is as dangerous as football.

tennis	difficult	English	nice	comics	funny
swimming	expensive	German	useful	books	interesting

8 What girls whisper

Schau dir diese Mädchen an. Sie reden über Mike, aber er kann nicht alles hören. Kannst du einfügen, was sie sagen? Benutze die Adjektive *tall, strong, silly, bad, good, nice* in ihren verschiedenen Formen.

He is very tall. I think he's ________ ______________ boy in our class.	Is he? No, I think David is ________ ________ him.
And he's so strong. He must be ____ _______________ boy in our class.	He is very nice. I think he is even __________ than Tom.
Look at his hair. It has got the same colour ________ your hair. Have you got the same shoes, too?	Oh, don't be stupid; or you'll get a prize for _____________ question.
Is he good at maths? Do you think he can help me? I need somebody who is ___________________ Tom. You know, at maths Tom is even ___________________ me.	Why don't you go and ask him? He looks a bit silly, but perhaps he is ____________________ at maths ________ he looks.
Have you seen any of his photos? Anne told me his photos are ______ _______ photos she has ever seen.	Did he take any photos of Anne? Then they must be _____________. She always thinks she's _________ ________ girl in our class.

9 What about your training?

Du bist bald fertig mit diesem Buch. Kannst du ein paar Fragen beantworten?

1. Has your English become ______________ (good) ?
2. Let's hope it hasn't become ______________ (bad).
3. Is the number of mistakes in your English tests ______________ or ______________ (small/big) than before?
4. Were the exercises very ______________ (boring) ?
5. Were they ____________________________________ (interesting) than in your textbook?
6. Were they ____________________ (boring) as in your textbook?
7. Or were they ______________ (bad) ?
8. Was the grammar ______________ (clear) enough?
9. Or was the grammar in your textbook ______________ (easy) ?
10. We hope that you didn't find things too ___________________ (difficult).

1

Welche Form hat das Adjektiv?

a) York is one of the ____________ cities in England. **(old)**

b) It was, together with London, the ____________________________ town in Roman times. **(important)**

c) York has many monuments. It has, for example, the ______________ medieval* Cathedral in Northern Europe. **(large)**

d) It has many good museums, too. The Jorvic Viking Centre is one of the ________________________________ museums about Viking history. **(interesting)**

e) There is the railway museum, too. It is ______________________ **(big)** railway museum in the world.

f) The countryside around York is very beautiful. It offers one of __________ __________________________ sights in Northern England. **(beautiful)**

2

Vergleiche "the two Yorks".

a) New York is much ______________________ York. **(big)**

b) York's population isn't ________________ **(mixed)** ______ New York's population.

c) York is much ____________ ____________ New York. **(old)**

d) New York's history isn't ________ old ________ York's, but it is certainly ________________________________ . **(interesting)**

e) New York's climate is different. It's much ____________ in summer and much ____________ in winter **(hot/cold)**.

f) There is more money in New York today ____________ in York. Most people are ____________, but there are also many people who are ____________. **(rich/poor)**

*medieval – mittelalterlich

18 Adverbien

18.1 Adverbien der Art und Weise

Wenn du sagen willst, wie man etwas tut – ob schnell, langsam, gründlich usw. –, verwendest du ein Adverb, und zwar ein Adverb der Art und Weise. Solche Adverbien gibt es auch im Englischen *(adverbs of manner)*.

Im Deutschen haben die Adverbien oft die gleiche Form wie das entsprechende Adjektiv. Im Englischen musst du dagegen zwischen zwei verschiedenen Formen unterscheiden.

Adverb	**Adjektiv**
Sie singt **schön**.	Ihre Stimme ist **schön**.
She sings **beautifully**.	Her voice is **beautiful**.

Du bildest die Adverbien, indem du an das Adjektiv ein -**ly** anhängst:

bad + **ly**	→	bad**ly**
careful + **ly**	→	careful**ly**
nice + **ly**	→	nice**ly**

Beachte:

- Bei Adjektiven, die auf Konsonant + **y** enden, wird das **y** zu **i**:

happ**y** + **ly**	→	happ**ily**
nois**y** + **ly**	→	nois**ily**

- Adjektive, die auf -**ble** enden, verlieren das -**le**:

terri**ble** + **ly**	→	terri**bly**

- **Good, hard, fast** haben unregelmäßige Adverbformen:

Tom is a good singer.	He sings **well**.
Mike is a fast runner.	He runs **fast**.
Jenny is a hard worker.	She works **hard**.

1 Tom's class

Trage die Adverbien ein.

1. Betty is a good dancer. She dances ______________________.
2. Kevin is a fast runner. He runs ______________________.
3. Ann has a beautiful voice. She sings ______________________.
4. Susan is a quiet girl. She does everything ______________________.
5. Jim is a very noisy boy. He always runs around ______________________.
6. Barbara is a hard worker. She works ______________________.
7. Kate is a clever girl. She always answers ______________________.
8. John is a happy boy. He always laughs ______________________.
9. Jane is a terrible dancer. She dances ______________________.
10. Matthew is very good at German. He speaks German very

    ______________________.

2 What can you do, what can your friends do?

Zähle auf, was du tun kannst. Dann berichte, was dein Freund/deine Freundin ist oder tun kann. Verwende Adjektive und Adverbien.

Beispiel: a) I am good at English. I can speak English very well.
b) My friend …

noisy *fast* *hard* *easy*
slow *careful* *clever*
intelligent *bad* *excellent* *quick*
nice *boring* *exciting* *wonderful*

18.2 Adjektiv oder Adverb?

Um entscheiden zu können, ob ein Adjektiv oder ein Adverb steht, solltest du dir folgende Grundregeln einprägen.

Adjektive beziehen sich immer auf Pronomen und Substantive. Vor einem Substantiv steht daher immer ein Adjektiv und nie ein Adverb:

He is a **careful** worker. He is a **dangerous** driver.

Adverbien der Art und Weise geben an, wie etwas getan wird. Sie beziehen sich daher immer auf ein Verb:

He works **carefully**. He drives **dangerously**.

Ist *to be* das Verb eines Satzes, steht immer ein Adjektiv:

She **is clever** and **intelligent**.

3 A fire at school

Adjektiv oder Adverb? Was ist richtig?

All the children were _______________ (quiet) sitting in the classroom when suddenly they heard a siren. What was it? Could it be one of those _______________ (silly) fire alarms? Then they all saw it. Smoke was coming out in _______________ (thick) clouds from the main building and in one room they saw _______________ (red) flames. They were all very _______________ (excited) and immediately wanted to leave the classroom. "Be _______________ (quiet) and sit down," the teacher shouted _______________ (angry). "You needn't be _______________ (afraid). Remember what you must do when there is a fire alarm. You Pete, you get up _______________ (quick) and shut these windows. Then let's leave the room, but don't run: let's leave it _______________ (slow) and in _______________ (good) order. Keep together and remember to shut the door _______________ (careful). Leave your things in the room if you can't pack

them ______________ (quick). Are you all ______________ (ready) ?
So let's get out ______________ (slow) now. Jane, don't forget the register.
Jimmy, you are the last; be ______________ (sure) to shut the door behind you."

4 Chaos at school

Als alle im Flur waren, sahen die Lehrer viele Dinge, die ihnen nicht gefielen. Adjektiv oder Adverb? Was gehört in die Lücken?

1. Lots of windows and doors were still ______________ (open).
2. Some pupils were running around ______________ (excited) in the corridor.
3. Others were still ______________ (quiet) packing their things.
4. One pupil was ______________ (busy) copying his homework from his friend's exercise book. He wasn't even writing very ______________ (fast).
5. Another pupil was reading a comic. He didn't think it was ______________ (dangerous) to remain in the building.
6. Some were ______________ (excited) watching the smoke from the windows of their classrooms.
7. Others were ______________ (happy) that there was a fire at their school.
8. A ______________ (good) fire is less ______________ (boring) than an English lesson, one of them said ______________ (excited).
9. And there will be no English tomorrow, somebody else added ______________ (quick).

18.3 Die Stellung von Adverbien der Art und Weise

Wenn du Adverbien der Art und Weise verwendest, musst du auf die Satzstellung aufpassen.

Adverbien der Art und Weise stehen nach dem Verb, wenn kein Objekt vorhanden ist:

They talked **quickly**. He listened **excitedly**. He smiled **happily**.

Ist ein direktes Objekt vorhanden, so steht das Adverb meist nach diesem Objekt:

They left the room **quietly**. They shut the door **quickly**.

Ist das Adverb weniger betont, kann es auch vor dem Verb stehen:

They **quietly** left the room.

Beachte:
Im Unterschied zum Deutschen darf im Englischen **nie** ein Adverb zwischen dem Verb und dem direkten Objekt stehen!

5 Helping hands ...

Bald hörten die Schüler ein anderes Geräusch. Es war die Sirene eines Feuerwehrautos, das in den Schulhof einbog. Setze die Adverbien an die Stelle, an die sie hingehören.

quick, careful, worried, nervous, excited, busy, fast

1. Four men jumped out of it.
2. Two of them ran into the building.
3. They raised a ladder.
4. One man climbed up the ladder.
5. Another man fetched the water hose.
6. "Where can we take the water from?" one man asked.
7. "Where do we begin?" one man asked.

1

Adjektiv oder Adverb? Trage die richtige Form ein.

a) When there is a fire, don't be ____________________ (nervous), don't run around ____________________ (excited), but keep cool and pack your things ____________________ (quick), or better leave them where they are.

b) Shut all windows and doors ____________________ (careful), see that nobody is left behind and leave the room as ____________________ as you can. (fast)

c) Don't panic when you see the smoke or the fire, but try ________________ not to get excited (hard).

d) Follow the instructions of the firemen ____________________ (careful) and leave the building immediately.

e) Make a ___________ job out of a ___________ thing. (good/bad)

2

Am nächsten Tag musste Toms Klasse über das Feuer schreiben. Hier sind ein paar Auszüge aus den Aufsätzen. Wähle ein passendes Adjektiv aus, bilde das Adverb und schreibe die Sätze neu mit den Adverbien.

excited *nervous* *bad* *deep*
fast *loud* *hard*
stupid *quiet* *terrible* *quick*

a) I was sitting in the classroom when suddenly the alarm bell rang. First I didn't know what do do, but then I understood the danger we were in.
b) The firemen did a good job and managed to put out the fire.
c) Teachers and pupils were running around.
d There were quite a lot of pupils who behaved …
e) I ran along the corridor with the other pupils of my class; we shouted, "Fire, fire!"
f) My neighbour coughed when the smoke got into his lungs.

19 Die Wortstellung im Englischen

19.1 Die Stellung des Subjekts im Aussagesatz

Da englische Substantive außer der Pluralendung keine Endungen haben, liegt die Wortstellung im Englischen fest. Du kannst sie daher nicht einfach ändern, ohne dass sich auch der Sinn des Satzes ändert:

The dog bites the postman.
The postman bites **the dog**.

Wie du aus diesem Beispiel siehst, bestimmt im Englischen die Wortstellung die Funktion eines Substantivs (oder Pronomens): Steht es in einem Aussagesatz vor dem Verb, ist es Subjekt. Steht es nach dem Verb, ist es Objekt des Aussagesatzes. Aus diesem Grunde sind auch andere Umstellungen, die du vom Deutschen her kennst, im Englischen nicht möglich.

Im englischen Aussagesatz steht das Subjekt **immer** vor dem Verb. Es wird auch dann nicht umgestellt, wenn ihm ein anderer Satzteil vorausgeht.

Heute **habe ich** Kopfweh. Today **I have got** a headache.
Heute **bin ich** krank. Today **I am** ill.

1 A week in Jenny's life

Jenny trägt immer in ihren Kalender ein, was passiert oder was sie vorhat. Schau dir ihren Kalender an und frage sie dann nach ihren Eintragungen.

Beispiel: What are you going to do on Monday, Jenny?
Well, let me see … On Monday, I …

Monday:	4 p.m. table tennis with Tom
Tuesday:	8.15 p.m. watch film on TV
Wednesday:	after school learn for German test with Tom
Thursday:	6 p.m. help Kate with maths homework
Friday:	5 p.m. buy birthday present for Sarah/ring up Sarah
Saturday:	Sarah's birthday party at 2 p.m.
Sunday:	ring up Tom/go for a walk with Tom at 4 p.m.

2 Tom's homework

Als Hausaufgabe in Deutsch musste Tom acht Sätze schreiben. Hier sind sie. Kannst du sie ins Englische übersetzen?

1. *Heute bin ich krank.*
2. *Heute muss ich nicht aufstehen.*
3. *Heute kann ich im Bett bleiben.*
4. *Heute muss ich nicht in die Schule gehen.*
5. *Heute muss ich keine Hausaufgaben machen.*
6. *Heute habe ich kein Deutsch.*
7. *Heute habe ich Fieber.*
8. *Heute ist ein schöner Tag.*

19.2 Die Stellung von Objekten, Orts- und Zeitangaben

Stellung der Objekte

Wenn das indirekte Objekt (wem?) nicht besonders betont ist, steht es gewöhnlich vor dem direkten Objekt (wen oder was?). Folgt es dem direkten Objekt, muss ein *to* vor das indirekte Objekt gestellt werden.

Subjekt	**Verb**	**(ind. Objekt)**	**dir. Objekt**	**(ind. Objekt)**
Tom	has got		a sister.	
He	likes		her.	
She	likes		ice cream.	
He	gives	her	an ice cream.	
He	gives		an ice cream	to his sister.
He	gives	Timmy	an ice cream.	

Beachte:
Objekte stehen im Englischen **immer nach** dem Verb oder der Verbgruppe. Im Englischen dürfen keine Satzteile zwischen dem Verb und dem Objekt stehen.

Stellung von Orts- und Zeitangaben

Zeitangaben stehen meist am Ende des Satzes. Wenn sie am Satzanfang stehen, sind sie stärker betont. Auch Ortsangaben können am Satzanfang stehen.

Wenn Zeit- und Ortsangaben zusammentreffen, steht die Ortsangabe **immer vor** der Zeitangabe:

Zeit/Ort			**Ort**	**Zeit**
	Tom	gets up		at 6.30.
	He	goes	to school	after breakfast.
Today	he	walks	to school.	
In England	school	starts		at 8.30.

3 Where's my money?

Als Sarah ihre Pommes frites bei Mrs Owen bezahlen will, stellt sie fest, dass sie kein Geld dabei hat. Sie fragt ihre Freundinnen, ob sie ihr welches leihen können. Setze bitte ein, was sie sagen.

Mrs Owen: So, here you are. That's £ 2.30.

Sarah: Oh, dear. Where have I put my purse?
Did I give ____________________, Christine?

Christine: No, you didn't. But perhaps you gave ___________ Sandra.
Sandra, have you got it?

Sandra: No, I haven't. Perhaps you left it at home.

Sarah: Maybe. Can any of you lend ___________ some money?

Christine: Sorry, I can't. I've already lent __________________ Tom and he hasn't given it back yet.

Sandra: Sorry, Sarah. I've just got enough money on me to pay for my chips.

Sarah: Well then, no lunch for me today. Sorry, Mrs Owen.

Mrs Owen: No need to worry, Sarah. I know you. You can have your chips and bring __________________ tomorrow.

Sarah: Thanks, Mrs Owen. I won't forget to __________________ back _________ you.

19.3 Die Stellung von Adverbien der Häufigkeit

Unter Adverbien der Häufigkeit versteht man Ausdrücke wie *often, always, sometimes, never, usually, seldom, mostly* u. a. Sie geben an, wie oft man bestimmte Dinge tut.

Im Unterschied zum Deutschen stehen Adverbien der Häufigkeit im Englischen **nie** zwischen Verb und Objekt.

Die Adverbien der Häufigkeit stehen:

- im *simple present* und im *simple past* vor dem Verb.

  Last year Mike **often did** his homework at school.
  This year he **usually does** it at home.

- bei Hilfsverben, denen ein Infinitiv oder ein *past participle* folgt, nach dem Hilfsverb.

  He **must always** help his sister.
  She **has never** done his homework.
  She **will never** do it.

- im *simple present* und *simple past* nach den Formen von *to be*, sonst nach dem Hilfsverb.

  Timmy **isn't often** ill.
  He **was sometimes** ill last year.
  But he **has never** been really ill.

Beachte:
Sometimes kann auch am Satzanfang stehen, wenn es besonders betont ist:

Sometimes Tom forgets his homework.

4 Homework

Bilde Sätze mit *often, usually* usw.

There are pupils

- who forget their homework. (usually)
- who have forgotten their homework. (never)
- who do their homework at school. (often)
- who have copied it from their neighbours. (never)
- who know what they must do. (never)
- who write down what they must do. (never)
- who forget their homework at home. (always)
- who do it on the way to school. (usually)
- who leave their exercise book at home. (sometimes)
- who forget it on the bus. (sometimes)

5 You and your homework

Antworte in ganzen Sätzen. Verwende dabei *always, often* usw.

1. What about your homework? Do you usually do it?
2. When do you usually do it?
3. Where do you do it?
4. Do you often forget it?
5. Why do you sometimes forget it?
6. Do you often copy it from your neighbour?
7. Are you usually busy in the breaks?
8. Must your neighbour/your mum/your dad often help you with your homework?
9. In what subjects must he or she often help you?
10. Has your teacher ever helped you?

6 Schools in England

Englische Schulen sind zum Teil anders. Lies dir die folgenden Sätze durch und schreibe sie richtig aus. Beachte dabei die Wortstellung!

1. go already/English pupils/when they are five/to school
2. go to a comprehensive school/most English pupils/when they are eleven.
3. when they are 16/school/they can leave
4. school uniforms/in many schools/they must wear
5. are blue and grey/the school colours/in Tom's school
6. the school uniforms/in special shops/can buy/the pupils' parents
7. later than in Germany/in most English schools/begin lessons
8. lessons/in the afternoon/most English pupils have/also
9. school cafeterias/many English schools/so/there are lessons also in the afternoon/ have
10. lunch/pupils/can have/during lunch break/at the school cafeteria
11. In many English schools/learn/pupils/to cook

7 What you can do or say

Schreibe zehn Sätze. Beginne mit dem Nebensatz.

Beispiel: Before I go to school, I usually do my homework.

What do you	say do think	before you go to school? when you don't want to go to school? when it's too cold to get up? when you are late? when you must do your homework? when you must go to bed? before you get up? before you have breakfast? when you go to bed? when you can't find your homework?

1

Ergänze die fehlenden Adverbien.

a) Today, I'll play football. I play football on Friday. (usually)

b) On Mondays, I go to the cinema. (sometimes)

c) After school, I go to Tom. (often)

d) What we do there? We play games or do our homework. (usually)

e) Do you play with Kate, too? No, we play with Kate. (seldom)

f) What I do in the evening? When I'm at home, I watch TV. (often)

g) If I watch TV with my parents? Yes, I do. (usually)

h) If my parents are out? (often) You can't tell; they are or they aren't. (sometimes)

i) When I go to bed? I go to bed at 10. (always)

j) When I get up? I get up at 7. (usually)

k) If I am late? (often) No, I'm not. I'm late. (never)

2

Verbessere die Wortstellung in den folgenden Sätzen.

a) As you know, are German schools from English schools different.

b) Pupils start usually school at the age of 6 or 7.

c) In Germany start lessons earlier than in England.

d) In most cases are German schools no all-day schools.

e) Usually German pupils have at home lunch.

f) No school cafeterias have most German schools.

g) So spend German pupils not so much time at school.

h) They usually are in the early afternoon at home.

20 Notwendige Relativsätze

Was versteht man eigentlich unter Relativsätzen und welche Aufgabe haben sie? Schau dir mal die folgenden Beispiele an:

Let's talk about *the girl* **Mike likes.**
Look at *the photo* **which is lying on the table.**
This is *a photo* **he likes very much.**

Wenn du z. B. im ersten Satz den fett gedruckten Satzteil zudeckst oder weg denkst, dann ist es nicht mehr völlig klar, um welches Mädchen es sich handelt. Wenn du jedoch wissen willst, was das für ein Mädchen ist, brauchst du eine zusätzliche Information. Diese zusätzliche Information liefert der Relativsatz: Er bestimmt die Person oder die Sache näher, auf die er sich bezieht und macht sie so für den Hörer verständlich. Daher stehen Relativsätze auch immer unmittelbar nach dem Substantiv, auf das sie sich beziehen.

Die Relativpronomen *who* und *which*

Notwendige Relativsätze werden oft durch *who* und *which* eingeleitet. Dabei steht *who* für Personen und *which* für Dinge.

This is the girl **who** lives in Kent Street.	**Subjekt**
This is the girl (**who**) Mike likes.	**Objekt**
Look at the photo **which** is lying on the table.	**Subjekt**
That's the photo **(which)** Mike likes best.	**Objekt**

Sind *who* oder *which* Subjekt des Relativsatzes, können sie nicht ausgelassen werden. Sind *who* und *which* dagegen Objekt des Relativsatzes, lässt man sie oft weg. Man spricht dann von *contact clauses,* da die Relativsätze unmittelbar an das Bezugswort angehängt werden. *Contact clauses* sind vor allem in der Umgangssprache häufig.

Achtung:
Bei notwendigen Relativsätzen steht im Englischen kein Komma!

1

Define the following nouns

Beispiel: A baker / make bread — A baker is a man who makes bread.

1. a pilot / fly a plane

   ____

2. a nurse / look after people who are ill

   ____

3. a doctor / examine sick people

   ____

4. a vet / look after sick animals

   ____

5. a shopkeeper / have got a shop

   ____

6. a shop assistant / work in a shop

   ____

7. a car mechanic / repair cars

   ____

8. a customer / buy things

   ____

9. a mother / have children

   ____

10. a bus driver / drive bus

    ____

2 Definitions ...

Verbinde die Satzteile. Verwende dabei *"who"* oder *"which"*.

A girl	is somebody	makes you sad.
A teenager	is something	asks too many questions.
A test		is lazy and loud.
A pupil		can be a problem.
School		talks a lot.
A teacher		isn't a baby anymore.
A school report		makes you learn a lot of silly things.
A mother		makes my parents cry.
A bad mark,		

somebody = who something = which

3 Hobby horses

Lass das Relativpronomen weg, wo es nicht notwendig ist.

1. Tom hasn't got a real hobby, but there are many things ___________ he likes.
2. He likes school, but he doesn't like all the subjects ___________ he must take.
3. Mike likes girls, but he doesn't like all the girls ___________ are in his class.
4. Kate likes sleeping. Her bed is the piece of furniture ___________ she likes best.
5. Jenny likes pets. The pet ___________ she has got is a hamster.
6. Her friend likes pop music. She collects all the CDs ___________ she can buy.
7. Timmy likes picture books. He can colour all the pictures ___________ he sees in them.
8. Mike likes taking photos. He puts the photos ___________ he has taken in an album, too.
9. John likes food. The food ___________ is on his plate looks good.
10. Mr Mason likes working on the farm ___________ he has got.

1

Vervollständige die folgenden Sätze.

1. A pupil is somebody …	who	doesn't eat meat.
2. A classmate is …	which	can be very funny.
3. A test …		looks like my teacher.
4. A monster …		can be very interesting.
5. A game …		still goes to school.
6. A vegetarian …		can be a problem.
7. Football …		is in your class.

2

Setze das richtige Relativpronomen ein. Bilde *contact clauses*.

Do you like all the pupils who are in your class?

Are there any girls who you like?

Are there any pupils who you can't stand?

Are there any pupils who don't like you?

Are there any pupils Who are afraid of you?

Is there anything wich you do together after school?

Are there any games wich you play together?

What are the games wich you like best?

3

Bilde Relativsätze. Ersetze dabei das Personalpronomen durch das entsprechende Relativpronomen. Bilde, wenn möglich, *contact clauses*.

1. Jenny is the girl. Tom likes her best.

   Jenny is the girl Tom likes best.

3. Most of the other boys and girls like her, too. They are in her class.

   Most of the other boys and girls who are in her class like her.

4. There are only few people. They don't like her.

   There are only few people

5. The teachers like her, too. They know her.

Lösungen

Allgemeiner Hinweis:
In den Lösungen wurde bei den Hilfsverben und den Formen von *to be* und *to do* nur eine mögliche Antwort angegeben. Sowohl die Langformen (*she is, cannot, is not, does not* usw.) als auch die Kurzformen (*she's, can't, isn't, doesn't* usw.) sind als richtig zu betrachten.

1 Substantive

1

a) There are Mr Mason, his wife and a farmworker on the farm. There are a cock and a few geese, some hens, a cat, a dog and some pigs on the farm, too.

b)

nouns in the singular	*nouns in the plural*
a farmhouse	some farmhouses
a wife	some wives
a dog	some dogs
a pig	some pigs
a cock	some cocks
a hen	some hens
a goose	some geese
a chimney	some chimneys
an apple tree	some apple trees

2

a cat – a bull – a cow – a dog – a horse – a pony – a mouse – a goose

3

There are a lot of men, women and children – presents – two boys – hand – present – teddy – one foot – one arm – one eye – mice – cake

4

1. This is a boy and these are boys, too.
2. That is a car and those are cars, too.
3. This is a street and these are streets, too.
4. That is a house and those are houses, too.
5. This is a brush and these are brushes, too.
6. That is a baby and those are babies, too.
7. This is a foot and these are feet, too.

5

trousers – shoes – clothes – clothes – jeans – tights

6

are – them – They are – It is – are

7

a) I'm wearing … b) I like … best.

Test

1

singular	*plural*
a horse	some horses
a hen	some hens
a goose	some geese
a duck	some ducks
a rabbit	some rabbits
a boy	some boys
a girl	some girls
a child	some children
a teddy	some teddies
a man	some men
a woman	some women
a house	some houses
a brush	some brushes
an apple	some apples
a sandwich	some sandwiches

2

these old things – this old pullover – it – They – they – They – them

3

presents – photos – people – those two big boxes – homework

2 Das Personalpronomen

1

1. **He** is on the farm.
2. **She** is in the house.
3. **He** is at school.
4. **It** is at school, too.
5. **He** is on his potty.
6. **They** are on the floor.
7. **They** are on his bed.
8. **She** is not at home.
9. **She** is with her.
10. **They** are in the park.

2

1. I can't find **them**.
2. I can't find **it**.
3. I can't see/hear **you**.
4. I can't see **him**.
5. I can't see **them**.
6. I can't find **them**.
7. I can't find **them**.
8. I can't find/see **it**.
9. I can't find **him**.
10. I can't see **it**.
11. I can't see/find **it**.
12. I can't see/find **them**.

3

Kate: me – them – they
Timmy: they – they
Kate: they – me – they
Timmy: they – They are
Kate: it
Timmy: It's
Kate: they
Timmy: them

Test

1

Lösungsvorschläge:

Where are Tom and Mike? They are in the classroom/here/on the bus/at school. Where is your homework? It's here/on the bus/at home/in my schoolbag … Where is your English book? It's on the desk/here/at home … Where is your book? It's in my schoolbag/at home/here … Where is Christine? She's in the classroom/here/at home/not here … Where is the register? It's on the desk/in my schoolbag/on the bus … Where are they from? They're from York. Where are you from? I'm from … Where is Kate? She's not here/at home/in the classroom …

2

When I've got a dog, I must wash it/brush it/talk to it/look after it.
When I've got a lot of homework, I must forget it.

When I've got dirty clothes, I must wash them.
When I've got a silly neighbour, I must talk to him/her.
When I've got a baby, I must look after him/her.
When I've got a friend, I must be nice to him/her.
When I've got a new computer game, I must try it.
When I've got problems, I must talk about them.
When I've got a good book, I must read it.

Bestimmter und unbestimmter Artikel 3

1

[ðɪ]	[ðə]
old women	yellow apples
English children	wrong numbers
examples	young girls
afternoons	silly answers
easy units	bad ideas
American cars	difficult questions
empty pages	school uniforms
	terrible teachers

2

Jenny isn't Tom's sister, she is Tom's friend – in Apple Street – Apple Street is – in the north of York – to school by bus – to school by bike – Tom is – all the girls and boys – she likes Tom – the nicest boy – like Tom – likes maths – Maths is the subject – Before tests – helps Tom

3

Lösungsvorschläge:
I can go to Germany by plane/by train …
I can go to New York by plane/by boat …
I can go to Scotland by train/by car/by taxi/by bike/by motorbike/on foot …
I can go to Ireland by plane/by boat …
I can go to Denmark by plane/by boat …
I can go to France by plane/by train/by ferry …
I can go to the Isle of Wight by boat/by train …
I can go to Wales by train/by plane/by bus/by car …
I can go to California by plane.

4

1. Boys like girls.
2. Tom likes Jenny.
3. Do you like the boys in your class?
4. Do you usually like girls more than boys?
5. What about the girls in your class?
6. Which of the boys/girls do you like best?
7. Who is the nicest boy/girl in your class?
8. What's the name of the girl/boy you like best?
9. Which boy/girl do most of you like best?
10. Are the boys/girls in your class good at English?
11. Are boys as clever as girls?

5

an English book – a workbook – an exercise book – a German book – a pencil case – an apple – an empty bottle – a water pistol – an old sandwich

6

1. He's a **milkman**.
2. He's a **postman**.
3. He's a **butcher**.
4. He's a **greengrocer**.
5. She's a **shop assistant**.
6. She's a **reporter/journalist**.
7. He's a **fireman**.
8. He's a **vet**.
9. He's a **teacher**.
10. He's a **burglar**.

7

an old woman – a young girl – an American car
an English child – a silly answer – a difficult question
an example – a bad idea – a school uniform
a yellow apple – an afternoon – an empty page
a wrong number – an easy unit – a terrible teacher

8

Jenny goes to the same school as Tom – takes them to school in the morning – The school they go to is a big school – a lot of pupils – like school – she likes school – most of the teachers – she can't go to school – stay in bed – she hasn't got a temperature – a cold – a bad headache – a doctor – stay in bed

Test

1

Tom has got a brother and a sister. They live in York. That's in the north of England. Timmy … Tom has got a grandpa and a grandma, too. – He has got a farm, so he is a farmer. Tom and Kate go to school. – He's too young to go to school. It's sometimes hard for Tom and Kate to get out of bed … Tom usually goes to school by bike. He only takes the bus … Kate goes to school by bus. She mustn't go by bike … Tom and Kate don't like everything about school, but most of their teachers are nice.

2

Lösungsvorschläge:

I live in …
I live in … Street.
I'm …
I've got/I haven't got …
My father/mother is a …
I like school/I don't like school because …
I like … best.
I hate …
My teachers are …
In winter/summer I get to school by …
I like better to go to school by …
My father/mother goes to work by …

4 Substantive und ihre Begleiter

1

1. It's **their** flat.
2. It's **their** car.
3. It's **his** sister.
4. It's **her** brother.
5. They are **his** toys.
6. It's **his** camera.
7. It's **her** boyfriend.
8. It's **their** school.
9. It's **their** house.

2

1. I think they are **his** keys.
2. It's not **your** exercise book, it's Kate's. It's **her** exercise book.
3. How can Jenny do Geman tests when you keep it under **your** bed? What will **her** teacher say?
4. This is not **your** picture book, it's Kate's. It was **her** birthday present from Tom.
5. Here's **your** teddy, here's **your** toy car, here's **your** telephone. So play with **your** things now.

3

1. your – you
2. you – your
3. your
4. your
5. you – your
6. you – your
7. you – your
8. you – your

4

There are a lot of things – There are – They are on the chairs – there is something – It's an old pullover – There are some socks – There are holes in them and they look dirty – There are a lot of photos – that photo over there – It's a photo – It's not a new bike, but its handlebars and its saddle are new.

5

Lösungsvorschläge:

Look at this classroom. There are ten desks. One of them is the teacher's desk. It is in front of the blackboard. There are a lot of exercise books, pencils and other things on the desks. There are some school bags on the floor. There is a map on the wall. It is a map of Great Britain and Ireland.

6

Timmy:	*Tom:*
Is **this** your classroom?	**This** isn't my classroom.
Is **this** your class?	Yes, **this** is my class.
And **that** class over there?	**That**'s Kate's class.
Is **this** your chair here?	… **that** chair over there, that's Jenny's.
What's the name of **that** fat boy over there?	
Is **that** a teacher over there?	
But **that** is a teacher, Tom.	Oh yes, **that**'s our English teacher.

7

There is room for 30 pupils. **There** are 30 chairs … and **there** is a desk. … **It's** a nice room. **There** are many pictures on the walls and **there** is a map of England, too. It's on the back, over **there**. My friend sits **there**. … but behind me, **there** are two girls … I don't like **them**. They … throw things at **me** and my friend. … they eat **their sandwiches** and **their** chocolate pudding and **their** sweets …

8

1. How much homework …
2. How much time …
3. How many minutes …
4. How many hours …
5. How many subjects …
6. How much help …
7. How many tests …
8. How many good marks …
9. How many tests …

9

a) When Tom comes home from school, he is always hungry. Usually there is **some** food for him in the fridge, but today it is empty. There is nothing in it. There isn't **any** butter, there isn't **any** bread, there isn't **any** jam or marmalade left. And there isn't **any** milk and **any** orange juice in it either. But there is a piece of paper on the table with **some** money on it. It reads: Sorry Tom, you must do the shopping today. There are **some** people waiting for me in my office. Buy yourself **some** food and buy **some** milk, too. And buy **some** orange juice for your sister. I hope the money is enough. Have you still got **any** left? Then take it. I must go to my bank first. See you later. Mum

b) There is **no** butter, there is **no** bread, there is **no** jam or marmalade left. And there is **no** milk and **no** orange juice in it either.

10

What am I going to eat? Some sausages perhaps? No, I won't have **any** sausages today. I had sausages yesterday.
An omelette then? Okay, but then I need three eggs and **some** milk. Are there **any** eggs left? Let me see. Yes, there are **some** eggs in the fridge.
And what about milk? Mum says that I must buy **some**. Then I'll buy **some**.
Do I need **anything** else? **Any** peas perhaps?
Have I got everything? Let's see … Oh, the money, of course. Where is my money? Oh yes, there's **some** money in my pocket. Is it enough? Yes, it is. Then I can buy **some** bottles of coke and **some** other things, too!

Test

1

a) Well, let me see **your** homework, John. Is this **your** homework or is it Kevin's homework? But why don't **you** tell me that **you** couldn't do it?
b) Where is **your** homework, Barbara? Can you show me **your** exercise book?
c) And what about **you**, Tom and Jenny? What are **you** doing over there? Are **you** copying **your** neighbours' homework?

2

1. Is **this** your pencil-case, Tom? No, it isn't. My pencil-case is over there.
2. What about **those** girls over there? Do you know them?
3. Yes, I know them. **This** girl is my sister and **that** girl is Jenny.
4. And the girl over there? Is **that** your girlfriend? No, silly, it isn't.

3

- much time
- many friends
- many books
- much fun
- much money

4

Do you know **any** pupils who have got problems at home? Well, I know **some**. **Some** of them have got really big problems. Kevin, for example, hasn't got **any** parents. And Jim's parents have got little or **no** money and Jim's mother is often ill. From time to time she must stay in hospital for **some** weeks.

Der Genitiv

1

Timmy's toys	the boys' teacher	the girls' school bags
our cat's food	Kate's friends	women's clothes
the man's boots	the children's books	the girls' school uniforms
Jenny's dog	the Masons' house	my parents' car

2

	Mögliche Antworten:
Are these your toys, Tom?	No, they aren't. They are my baby brother's.
Is this your girlfriend, Kevin?	No, it isn't. It's Tom's.
Is this your magazine, Jenny?	No, it isn't. It's the girls'.
Is this your cat, Kate?	No, it isn't. It's my mother's.
Is this your homework, Joe?	No, it isn't. It's Kevin's.
Is this your house, Mr Mason?	No, it isn't. It's my grandparents'.
Is this your bike, Mrs Mason?	No, it isn't. It's Kate's.
Is this your room, Tom?	No, it isn't. It's my sister's.
Is this your teddy, Jenny?	No, it isn't. It's Timmy's.

3

Tom's baby brother – one of his favourite toys – he's got (he has got) other toys, too – other things – there's (there is) one of Jenny's letters – there's (there is) an old German book and there's (there is) Kate's ruler – some keys – his parents' keys – there's (there is) a tennis ball – Is it Kevin's or Joe's – It can't be Kate's or Tom's …

4

s-Genitiv	*Kurzform*
Tom's girlfriend	She's (she is) twelve. She hasn't got … she's only got (she has only got) got her parents … it's (it is) her …
her grandparents' house	Jenny's other relatives she's got (she has got) an aunt who's (who is) over sixty and who's (who has got) got a flat … She hasn't got
Jenny's first visit to London	

5

the boys's legs	the girl's hands	the windows of the car
the doors of my room	the dog's feet	my neighbour's cat
Kate's books	the children's clothes	the end of school
on the evening of my birthday	the light of the moon	Jenny's story

6

Lösungsvorschläge:

a bar of chocolate
a glass of milk/tea
a cup of tea/coffee
lots of chocolate/food
a plate of strawberries
a tin of peas
a pound of cheese/sausages
a bag of food/crisps
a packet of cornflakes
a piece of cheese

7

five bags of crisps
three packets of biscuits
five bottles of coke
five bottles of lemonade
a bottle of tomato ketchup
three pounds of sausages
five packets of ice cream

8

Lösungsvorschläge:

Mrs White	*Tom*
	I need three packets of biscuits and five bags of crisps.
	I need some lemonade and some coke, too.
How many bottles do you want?	I need five bottles of lemonade and five bottles of coke.
Anything else?	Can I have some sausages, too?
How many do you need?	I need three pounds of sausages.
Anything else?	I need some ice cream, too.
How much do you want?	I need five packets of ice cream.

9

Get **off** that bike – on Tom**'s** bike – they will fall **off** the bike – So Mike takes one hand **out of** his pockets – not very far **from** the corner shop to the Masons' flat – the bottles fall **off** the bike – to Mrs White**'s** shop – both hands **out of** his pockets and no bottles fall **off** the bike – into Tom**'s** room – a phone call **from** Jenny**'s** mother – she's just come home **from** school – you will hear **from** her tomorrow.

Test

1

Lösungsvorschläge:

Tom's trousers/comics
Jenny's computer/room
Timmy's trousers/legs
women's magazines
my parents' room/computer

people's legs/magazines
children's magazines
a list of things
a bucket of milk
a packet of biscuits

2

lots of people – play games – there's always – some kind of fun – Tom's birthday party – some people – There's Jenny, there's Ann and there's his sister Kate – She's a very nice girl, not as silly as the other girls.

3

a) This plane is taking **off**.
b) This is a letter **from** London. It's **from** Jenny's aunt.
c) This boy is taking **off** his clothes. He's taking the money **out of** his pocket.
d) Where are you **from**?
e) Turn the lights **off**, please.
f) Is this one **of** your jokes?

6 *Have got, has got* und das *simple present* von *to be*

1

1. They **have got** a flat there.
2. Tom **has got** a room, and Kate **has got** a room, too.
3. Timmy **hasn't got** a room.
4. The Masons **have got** a car.
5. Tom and Kate **haven't got** a car, they **have got** bikes.
6. Timmy **hasn't got** a bike …
7. But he **has got** two big toy cars …

2

1. Kate hasn't got a sister/a boyfriend/a car/a toy car/a TV set, but she has got two brothers, a lot of friends/a bike/a lot of books/a football/a radio.
2. I have got …, but I haven't got …
3. My friend has got …/My friends have got …/He, she has got …/They have got …

3

Lösungsvorschläge:

Have you got a car? No, I haven't.
Has your mother got a water pistol? No, she hasn't.
Has your English teacher got a toy car? No, he hasn't.
Have your friends got a lot of toys? Yes, they have.

4

Today, it **is** Tom's birthday – He **is** twelve – All his friends **are** there – His sister **is** there – Her name **is** Kate – Only Jenny **is** not there – Where **is** she? – She is ill – All the children **are** – it **is** full of children – They **are** all hungry – There **are** a lot of sandwiches – there **are** some bottles – But one bottle **is** on the floor – it **is** broken – there **is** a pool – And who **is** in the pool? – It **is** Timmy …

5

1. No, it isn't. It's Tom's birthday.
2. No, she isn't. She is ill.
3. No, he isn't. He's twelve.
4. No, she isn't. She's Tom's friend/ girlfriend.
5. Yes, she is. She's his sister.
6. Yes, it is. It's Timmy.
7. Yes, there are. There are lots of sandwiches …

8. No, they aren't. They are in the kitchen.
9. Yes, they are. They are hungry and thirsty.
10. Yes, it is. One bottle is on the floor.

6

1. Who is Timmy?
2. Where is he?
3. Where is Mike from?
4. Where is Bristol?
5. Who is Jenny?
6. Where is she?
7. Where are Joe and Kevin?

7

Who is Jenny?
Is she from York?
Why isn't she here?
Are her parents at home?
How old is she?
Is she often ill?

Test

1

a) This **is** Kevin and that **is** Joe.
b) They **are** the best friends I **have got**.
c) And that boy over there **is** Bill.
d) He **is** in my class, too, and he **is** very good at maths.
e) And this **is** Ann. She**'s** Jenny's friend.
f) She **is** very sorry that Jenny can't **be** here.

2

a) Is it a thing ? No, it isn't.
b) Is it an animal? No, it isn't.
c) Is it in this room? No, it isn't.
d) Have you got it at home? No, I haven't.
e) Is it a person? Yes, it is.
f) Is it a man? Yes, it is.
g) Is it a teacher? Yes, it is.
h) Is he a terrible teacher? No, he isn't.
i) Has he got a dirty old car? Yes, he has.
j) Is it our English teacher? Yes, it is.

3

Why aren't you at Tom's party? I'm ill.

Are you really ill? Yes, I am.
What have you got? I've got a cold.
Are you unhappy that you can't come? Yes, I am.
Have you got a present for Tom?
Yes, I have.
Is it a football? No, it isn't.
What is it then? It's a secret.

7 Das *present progressive*

1

1. Mike is taking photos.
2. John is sitting at the table and drinking all the lemonade.
3. Kate is skipping.
4. Tom is ringing up Jenny.
5. Betty is flirting with Kevin.
6. Two boys are playing football in the kitchen.
7. Some girls are dancing in the kitchen.
8. Ann is lying on the floor and watching a film on TV.
9. Jim and Barbara are eating sandwiches.
10. Susan is sitting in a corner and reading a magazine.

2

1. That's not right, Timmy. Mike isn't playing with his camera, he's taking photos.
2. John isn't eating all the sandwiches, he's drinking all the lemonade.
3. Kate isn't hopping around like a rabbit, she's skipping.
4. Tom isn't talking to his teacher, he's talking to Jenny.
5. Betty and Kevin aren't kissing, they are talking.
6. They aren't quarrelling, they are playing football.
7. The girls aren't running around in the kitchen, they are dancing.
8. Ann isn't lying on the floor because she is ill. She's lying on the floor because she is watching a film on TV.
9. Jim and Barbara aren't making sandwiches, they are eating them.
10. Susan isn't reading your picture book, she is reading a magazine.

3

– Is John really eating all the sandwiches?	Yes, he is.
– Is Mike really playing with his camera?	Yes, he is.
– Is Kate really hopping around like a rabbit?	Yes, she is.
– Are some girls really running around in the kitchen?	Yes, they are.
– Is Susan really reading your picture book?	Yes, she is.
– Is Ann really lying on the floor because she is ill?	Yes, she is.

4

– What are you doing, Kate?	I'm skipping.
– Are you talking to your teacher, Tom?	No, I'm talking to Jenny.
– What are you doing with your camera, Mike?	I'm taking photos.
– Are you reading my picture book, Susan?	No, I'm reading a magazine.

- Why are you lying on the floor, Ann? I'm watching a film.
- Are you playing a new game, Kate? No, I'm not. It's an old game.
- What are you doing in the kitchen? We are playing football.
- And what are you doing in the kitchen? We are dancing.
- Are you still hungry, John? Yes, I am.

5

First scene:
When is the party over?
What is over at 7.30?
Where are the children going?
What are they?

Who is happy, too?
Where is he?

Who is lying on the floor?
Where is he lying?
What isn't he doing?
Who is playing with Tom's birthday presents?
Where are they now?
What is in the parcel?

Second scene:
Where is Timmy still lying?
What has he got in his hand?
Where is he drawing a picture?
What is he drawing?

Third scene:
Who is coming upstairs?
What is he shouting?
Who is it?
What is he doing?
What is he?
What is he opening?
What is empty?

Test

1

What is Betty doing? – **Who** is making a paper plane? – **What** are Tony and Tom doing? – **Where** is Jimmy lying? – **What** is Kate cleaning? – **What** are Pete and John playing? – **Who** is having his second breakfast? – **What** is Jim having? – **Where** is Mike running around?

2

What are you doing? Are you still flirting with Sue?
No, sir, I'm just asking her a question.
Are you still doing your homework?
I'm not doing my homework, sir. I'm taking notes.
John, why are you still eating?
And you Jimmy, why are you still crying? Look at the girls, they are laughing at you.
Are you all listening now?

8 Modale Hilfsverben

1

can – needn't – must – must – must – must – needn't – must – can't – must – must – can – can – can – mustn't – can

2

1. No, that's wrong. Kate can go to her room.
2. No, that's wrong. She needn't help.
3. No, that's wrong. Tom must help his mother to wash the dishes and to clean the kitchen floor, but he needn't clean Kate's room.
4. No, that's wrong. He must help to wash them up.
5. That's right.
6. That's wrong. He needn't clean them.
7. That's right. Timmy can help him with the dishes.
8. That's wrong. He needn't clean it.
9. That's wrong. He mustn't drop them.
10. That's right. He can stay up a little longer.

3

Tom:	*Jenny's mother:*
Can/may I talk to Jenny, please?	Sorry, Tom, you can't/may not.
Can Jenny come tomorrow?	No, she can't. She can't/may not/mustn't get up.
Must she stay in bed all day?	Yes, she must.
Must she take medicine?	No, she needn't.
Can/may I see her this afternoon?	No, you can't/may not see her today.
Can/may I see her tomorrow?	… you can/may ring her up again in the evening.

4

1. I mustn't go to school.
2. I must stay in bed for three days.
3. I must take my medicine.
4. I mustn't play with my friends.
5. I mustn't watch too much TV.
6. I must tell my mum to take my temperature every morning.
7. I must come to his surgery again on Monday at 4 o'clock.

5

She must take her medicine.
She mustn't ride on her bike.
She mustn't go to school.
She needn't do her homework.
She can ring up her friends.
She can write letters.
She needn't kiss her doctor.
She can watch TV.
She can read a book.
She needn't/mustn't clean her room.
She needn't/mustn't help her mother.
She can listen to music.
She mustn't play football.
She needn't wash her clothes.

6

1. No, you needn't.
2. Yes, you must.
3. No, you needn't.
4. Yes, you must.
5. No, you can't.
6. Yes, you can.
7. Yes, you must.
8. Yes, they may …
9. Yes, you can/may.
10. Yes, you must.

7

– Are you very ill?	Yes, I am.
– Must you stay in bed?	Yes, I must.
– Must you stay indoors all day?	Yes, I must.
– May you get up for an hour or two?	Yes, I may.
– Have you got a temperature?	Yes, I have.
– Can you go to school on Thursday?	No, I can't.
– Are you happy that you needn't go to school?	Yes, I am.
– Are your teachers happy, too?	No, they aren't.

8

1. He **needn't** go to school.
2. He **can** go to kindergarten.
3. He **can** play with other children there.
4. **Must** he go there every day?
5 No, he **needn't**.
6. **Can/may** he go there alone?
7 No, he **can't/may not/mustn't**.
8. **Can/may** he take his bike? No, he **can't/may not/mustn't**.
9. **Must** Tom fetch him in the afternoon?
10. Yes, he **must** fetch him on Thursdays and Fridays.

9

Shall I do the shopping for you?
Shall I clean the rooms?
Shall I go to the chemist's?
Shall I get your medicine?
Shall I cook the meals?
Shall I make an appointment?
Shall I do the washing up?
Shall I make your bed?
Shall I buy you some lemonade?
Shall I open the window?
Shall I ring up the doctor?
Shall I look after my sister/brother?

Test

1

a) A doctor must examine his patients.
b) He must take their temperature.
c) He must listen to what they tell him.
d) He must give them a prescription.
e) He must go and see his patients.
f) He must ask them how they feel.
g) He must send his patients to hospital when they are seriously ill.

2

a) A good patient must do what the doctor tells him/her.
b) A good patient must take his/her medicine.
c) A good patient must stay in bed when he/she is ill.
d) Correct.
e) Correct.
f) A good patient must listen to his/her doctor.

3

Mögliche Antworten:

- Shall I carry it for you?
- Shall I make you a sandwich?
- Shall I look for it?
- Shall I do it for you?
- Shall I clean them for you?
- Shall I help you?
- Shall I shut the windows?
- Shall I buy her a present?

Das *simple present* von Vollverben

1

1. He **gets up** …
2. Then he **washes** and **puts** on his clothes.
3. Then he **goes** down …
4. There he **has** breakfast.
5. Then he **looks** for his school bag.
6. After that he **leaves** the house.
7. Then he **goes** to the bus stop.
8. He usually **takes** the bus …
9. He **arrives** …
10. He **says** hello …

2

After school

- Tom goes home. He does his homework with Jenny; then they play games or watch TV.
- Kate goes to her room. She listens to music or she rings up her friends or plays.
- Mike sits in front of his computer. He plays computer games. He often forgets his homework.
- Ann and Barabara send SMS messages. Then they listen to music or read magazines.
- John has tea. He eats a lot of sandwiches. Then he lies down on his bed and has a nap.

3

1. They **don't get up** in the morning.
2. They **don't have** an early breakfast.
3. Mr Brown **doesn't wash** his car.
4. Mrs Brown **doesn't do** the cooking.
5. Often, their children **don't go** to school.
6. They **don't like** school.
7. Helen **doesn't like** her teachers.
8. She **doesn't do** her homework.

4

Tom likes bananas, but he doesn't like oranges.
He likes Jenny, but he doesn't like Ben.
Jenny and Kate like volleyball, but they don't like tennis.
They like sports, but they don't like all sports.
Timmy likes cornflakes, but he doesn't like tea.
He likes dogs, but he doesn't like cats.
Mike likes photos, but he doesn't like comics.
He likes music, but he doesn't like singing.
The Browns don't like work, but they like sleeping.
They don't like books, but they like TV.

5

Lösungsvorschläge:

I like tennis, but my mother doesn't.
I don't like maths, but my neighbour does.
My friends like pop music, but my parents don't.
My parents don't like Kate, but I do.

6

1. Do you like your new school?	Yes, I do.
2. Do you play football?	Yes, I do.
3. Does your sister go to our school, too?	Yes, she does.
4. Does she play tennis?	No, she doesn't.
5. Do you and your sister go to school by bike?	Yes, we do.
6. Do you play an instrument?	No, I don't.
7. Does your father work in York?	Yes, he does.
8. Does your mother like York?	Yes, she does.
9. Do your parents like it here?	Yes, they do.

7

1. Where do you live?	I live in …
2. When do you get up in the morning?	I get up at …
3. When does your mother get up?	She gets up at …
4. What do you have for breakfast?	I have … for breakfast.
5. Why don't you like cornflakes?	I don't like them because …
6. When do your parents leave the house?	They leave the house at …
7. When do they come home again?	They come home again at …
8. How do you get to school?	I get to school by …
9. Why don't you take the bus?	I don't take it because …
10. What do you do in the afternoon?	In the afternoon, I …
11. What games do you like?	I like …
12. What do you do in the evening?	In the evening, I …
13. When do you go to bed?	I go to bed at …
14. When do your parents go to bed?	They go to bed at …

8

Where does Mike live now?
What doesn't he like?
How does he go to school?
When does he leave the house?
Where does he usually arrive at 8.30?
Where does he have lunch?

When does his mother drive him to school?
What does his mother do?
When does the first lesson begin?

When does he get up?
What does he leave at a quarter to eight?
Why does he have lunch at school?
When does he often go to see Tom?
What do they play together until 6 or 7 o'clock?
What do they do?
Where does Mike go then?

9

1. When do you get up?
2. When do you start work?
3. When do you leave the house?
4. What do you drive?
5. Who do you collect from the villages?
6. Where do you take them?
7. When does school start?
8. When do you fetch them?
9. Where do you take them?
10. What do you clean then?
11. What do you often find in the bus?

Test

1

He goes …
She writes …
He uses …
He teaches …
She does …
She sees …
He closes …
He carries …
He loses …
This sounds …
He throws …
He loves …
She brushes …
He empties …
She wears …
He wants …
He takes …
He ties …
He misses …
He chooses …
She flies …

2

have – listen – does – make – talks – shows –find – talk – knows – have – listens – tries

3

When do you usually get home?
What do you usually do after school?
Do you like going to the cinema?
What kind of films do you like?
Do you often go to the cinema?
When do you do your homework?
How much time do you need for it?

10 *Simple present* und *present progressive*

1

This is Dad. He is sitting in the bus.
This is Dad again. He is cleaning the bus.
This is our house. We live there.
This is Mum. She is leaving the house. She always leaves at 8.
This is our garden. Look! Mum is working in it. She likes her garden.
This is our corner shop. Mum works there. She is selling something.

2

1. Mike usually **gets** up at 7, but today he is still in bed. He is **still sleeping**.
2. He usually **has** breakfast at 7.30, but today he is **still lying** in bed.
3. He often **has** no time to wash, but this morning he **is taking** a bath.
4. He usually **puts on** his school uniform, but today he **is wearing** different clothes.
5. He usually **has** lunch at school, but today he **is having** lunch at home.
6. Mike usually **helps** his mother, … His father **is washing** the dishes.
7. His parents usually **leave** the house … They **are going** for a walk.
   Do you know why? Well, it's **Sunday**.

3

Mögliche Antworten:
On Sundays I usually get up late/go for a walk/do my homework.
On Sundays I often watch TV/ring up my friends/play football/write letters.
On Sundays I sometimes help/Mum and Dad/brush my shoes.
On Sundays I never clean my room/clean my bike/go to school/learn English.
On Sundays I always play computer games/listen to CDs/go to Church.

4

Mr Mason usually gets up at seven o'clock. Then he washes and has breakfast. After that he gets in his car. He opens his surgery at 8.30. He examines sick animals between 9 and 12. Then he has lunch at a restaurant. At 5 p.m. he usually has a cup of tea. He closes the door of his surgery at 5.30. He usually comes home at 6.

5

Mögliche Antworten:

I get up at …, then I wash and have breakfast. Then I go to school. I usually come home at … In the afternoon I first …, then I … After that I … In the evenings I usually … I go to bed at …

6

First they break the eggs and put them in a bowl.
Then they add some milk, salt and pepper.
Then they stir the eggs.
Next they put fat in the frying pan.
Then they put everything in the frying pan.
After that they cook the eggs in the frying pan.
Then they put the scrambled eggs on a plate and eat them.

7

1. is shining – are still sitting
2. always have – is still missing – is sleeping
3. goes – opens – sees – tries – doesn't listen – goes back – tells
4. says – doesn't want
5. fetches – goes – is shouting

Test

1

a) Mike is **taking** a photo of his new school. He **likes** taking photos.
b) He **doesn't** only **take** photos of schools, he **takes** photos of everything.
c) He always puts his photos on a CD. Look! He **is putting** in a new CD now.
d) He **keeps** them in a desk.
e) Sometimes he **shows** them to his friends.

2

likes – learns – likes – wakes up – sits up – listens – is playing – jumps – rushes – switches – turns – goes – is sleeping – hears

11 Verneinung, Fragen und Kurzantworten

1

Lösungsvorschläge:

I think Jenny doesn't begin to cry.

I think she must laugh.

I think she writes a letter, too, and shows it to her neighbours.

I think Jenny is very unhappy.

I think she begins to cry and must leave the classroom.

I think she is very angry with him.

2

Mögliche Antworten:

1. That's wrong. Good pupils aren't silly.
2. That's wrong, too. Some of them do, but others don't.
3. That's wrong again. Some of them are bad at sports, but not all of them.
4. This is right. Good pupils usually don't forget their homework.
5. That's wrong. Sometimes they forget things, too.
6. That's wrong. Some of them make their teachers angry, too.
7. That's wrong again. Good pupils talk in lessons, too.
8. That's wrong. Some of them have a lot of friends, others don't.
9. That's wrong. There are good pupils who don't talk to their teachers.
10. That's wrong. Good pupils aren't unhappy, but sometimes bad pupils are.
11. That's wrong again. Good pupils are interested in other things, too.
12. That's wrong. There are good pupils who go out with their friends, too.
13. That's wrong again. Some of them do, but others don't.
14. That's wrong again. Also good pupils don't know everything.
15. That's wrong again. There are also good pupils who play computer games.

3

- Are you often alone?
- Do you like your parents?
- Have you got any friends?
- Have you got any hobbies?
- Do your parents often play with you?
- Have you got anybody to talk to?
- Do you watch a lot of TV?
- Are most of your teachers nice?
- Are you often afraid when you are alone?
- Are your parents often out in the evening?

4

- Can you sit still?
- Do you talk all the time?
- Can you listen?
- Do you listen only when your teacher gets angry?
- Do you often forget things?
- Do you do your homework?
- Do you find everything boring?
- Do you often sleep during lessons?
- Are you often late?
- Are you often ill for tests?
- Do you only like sports?

5

1. **Do** you **like** school?
2. **Do** you often **forget** your homework?
3. **Are** you **doing** your homework now?
4. **Is** your mum **helpin**g you now?
5. **Do** your parents often **help** you?
6. **Have** you **got** nice teachers?
7. **Do** they **like** you?
8. **Do** they g**ive** you a lot of homework?
9. **Can** you **talk** during lessons?
10. **May** you **eat** chewing gum in the English lessons?
11. **Have** you **got** a school magazine at your school?
12. **Do** you **read** it?
13. **Do** you **find** it interesting?

6

1. No, it isn't.
2. No, it isn't.
3. No, he isn't.
4. No, they aren't.
5. Yes, they are.
6. Yes, he is.
7. Yes, he does.
8. Yes, they are.
9. Yes, he is.
10. Yes, they do.
11. Yes, they do.
12. No, it isn't. It's a motorbike.

7

1. What building …?
2. How high …?
3. What is …?
4. Who are …?

5. What is leaning …?
6. How many people …?
7. What are they … ?
8. Who is running away … ?
9. Why are they … ?
10. Who are the two men?
11. Where is ….?
12. Who is …?
13. What is … ?

8

1. Who doesn't know the building?
2. What is very high?
3. What is leaning against the wall?
4. Who is running away?
5. Who is running to a bike?
6. Who is running after them?
7. Who wants to catch them?
8. Who hasn't got a uniform on?
9. Who is afraid of him?

9

1. Who is Tom's girlfriend?
2. Who is from Leeds?
3. What have they got?
4. Who is sometimes strict?
5. Who can't always see Tom? – Who can't she always see?
6. Who must she tell where she is going? – What must she tell her parents?
7. Who must be back early? – When must she be back?
8. When mustn't she be out?
9. What is ringing?
10. Who is at home? – Where is Tom?
11. Who is Jenny ringing up?
12. Who is very excited? – What is she?

10

Tom: What have you got?
What is it?
What do you like?
What must you buy for it?
Where must I come?
What must I lend you?
What do you want to buy?
Jenny: What is very bad?
Who can't you understand?

11

1. How old is he?
2. Where does he sleep?
3. When do you usually get up?
4. What do you do then?
5. What does he usually have for breakfast?
6. When do you take him for a walk?
7. When do you go for work?
8. Where do you take him then?
9. How long does he stay there?
10. Where do you play?
11. What do you try to teach him?
12. What do you do in the evening?
13. What films does he like?
14. Why does he like westerns?
15. What does he do when he sees them?
16. Why is he barking now?

Test

1

a) Jenny hasn't got a cat, she's got a hamster.
b) She doesn't keep it in her bedroom, she keeps it in a cage downstairs.
c) It doesn't sleep in her bed, it sleeps in its cage.
d) Jenny needn't talk to it a lot because it's not a budgie.
e) Tom needn't catch mice for it because it's not a cat.
f) She doesn't take it to school because her teachers don't like that.

2

a) Yes, I have/No, I haven't.
b) Yes, I do. No, I don't.
c) Yes, … has/No, nobody has.
d) Yes, they do/No, they don't.
e) Yes, you must.
f) No, I needn't.
g) No, it needn't.

3

a) Who has got a boyfriend? What has Jenny got?
b) Whose photo is on the wall? Where is his photo?
c) Who likes her? Who does he like?
d) Who likes him? Who does she like?
e) Who likes him, too? Who do they like?
f) Who is in the same class? Where are they?
g) Who often goes home together? Where do they often go together?
h) Who often rings her up? Who does Tom often ring up?
i) Who is sometimes happy? What are they sometimes?

12 Zeitformen zur Wiedergabe der Zukunft

1

1. I think the weather will be nice.
2. I don't think it will rain.
3. I hope we'll spend a nice day together there.
4. I hope the water won't be too cold.
5. If the water isn't too cold, we'll go for a swim.
6. I hope you'll have a good time.

2

Mögliche Antworten:

If the coach is late, they won't leave at 8 o'clock.
If it rains all day, they won't go to the beach.
If the sun doesn't shine, they won't go for a swim.
If some of the children are late, their teacher will be angry.
If their teacher is ill, there will be no excursion.
If there is too much traffic, they will be late.

3

	Mögliche Antworten:
When will we be there?	We'll be there at …
Will we need a warm pullover?	Yes, you will/No, you won't.
Will you buy us an ice cream?	Yes, I will/No, I won't.
Will we have lunch on the beach?	Yes, we will/No, we won't.
Will we play games on the beach?	Yes, we will.
Will we go back by bus or by train?	We'll go back by bus.
What games will we play?	We'll play …
Will we be allowed to walk around on our own?	No, you won't.
Will we have time enough to go shopping?	Yes, you will.
When will we be back?	We'll be back at …
Will our maths teacher come with us?	Yes, he will/No, he won't.

4

a) She hopes that the weather will be nice.
She hopes that it won't rain.
She hopes that she won't get a cold and fall ill.

She is sure that they will have lots of fun.
She hopes that her friends will go, too.
She is sure that they will see a lot of interesting things.
She thinks that her pocket money will be enough.
She hopes that there won't be too many teachers.
She hopes that there won't be any homework for the next day.

b) I hope the bus won't have a breakdown.
I hope our teachers will leave us alone.
I hope we won't have to visit that terrible museum.
Perhaps I'll find a nice present for my friend.

5

Lösungsvorschläge:

When they are on the beach, they will take off their clothes/they will play games/they will go for a swim/they will look for shells/they will splash their teacher with water/they will have a picnic on the beach/they will be very noisy/they will run around/they will rush into the water

6

Catherine: I'll buy something to drink, too.
Helen: I'll buy some, too.
Jim: Then I'll talk to her, too.
Ronny: Well, then I'll have a sandwich, too.

7

1. work
2. she is going to help her
3. going to invite him
4. is going to write him
5. are going to buy her a new bike.
6. What is she going to do? Well, she is going to clean it.
7. is going to go
8. is going to spend

8

1. What are you going to do about your tests, Kate? Are you going to work harder?
2. What are you going to do, Jenny? Are you going to help Kate?
3. What are you going to do, Kate? Are you going to invite Ben?
4. What are you going to do, Helen? Are you going to write Ben?
5. What are your parents going to do, Linda? Are they going to buy you a new bike?
6. What are you going to do with your room, Betty? Are you going to clean it?

7. What are you going to do in your holidays, Mary? Are you going to go to the seaside?
8. What are you going to do there? Are you going to spend your holidays there?

9

1. If the weather is fine, **we'll play** in the garden.
2. I think everybody **will like** that.
3. But I hope Ben **won't** come. I'm **not going to invite** him.
4. Perhaps Jenny **will** help me.
5. I hope Tom **will** help me with the lemonade. I **will** ask him when I see him.
6. Who **is going to** buy/**will** buy all the rest?
7. Well, **I'll ask** Mum … Perhaps he **will** be tired when he gets back.

10

1. We **won't** write it before next Monday. I think **I'll** start next Sunday.
2. **I'll** ask my father.
3. What **will** it be about? I think **I'll** have to ask John.
4. I don't think it **will** be very difficult. And I'm quite sure he **will** help me this time, too.
5. **I'll** be terribly nervous on Monday.
6. I'm **not going to** miss it. I **won't** go to school.

Test

1

Mögliche Antworten:
a) Then I'll do it for you.
b) I'll clean it for you.
c) I'll carry it for you.
d) I'll give/lend you some.
e) I'll look for it.
f) I'll try to find them/I'll look for them.
g) Oh, I'll kiss her for you.

2

a) Tomorrow we will write an English test.
b) I hope it won't be too difficult.
c) I hope my neighbour will help me.
d) Perhaps I'll get a good mark then.
e) I'm going to ask her tonight if she wants to help me.
f) If she helps me, I'll give her a bar of chocolate.
g) But I'll only give it to her if I my mark is good.
h) If my mark is bad, I'll eat the chocolate myself.

3

Mögliche Antworten:

I'm going to play football/help Mum/play computer games/go for a walk … I'm not going to go to school/play with my teddy/work for school/see my teacher …

Das *present perfect* 13

1

lived, carried, said, showed/shown, caught, brought, left, spent, written, kept, spoken, read, heard, given, played, lain, felt, thought, told, bought, stood, taken, found, known, made, begun

2

pay, choose, lose, throw, feed, sleep, wear, teach, fall, drop, try, buy, meet, run

3

- They have booked a place for July.
- They have written to the local tourist office.
- They have had a look at the road map.
- They have tried to find out the best route.
- They have begun to check their caravan.
- They have bought a new bottle of gas.
- They have checked the tyres.
- They have repaired the rear window.

4

We have washed the caravan, but we haven't cleaned the floor yet.
We have cleaned the windows, but we haven't made the beds yet.
We have put in some food, but we haven't bought a new frying pan yet.
We have put in Timmy's toys, but we haven't bought a new picture book yet.
We have taken Tom's tennis racket, but we haven't bought new tennis balls yet.
We have told the neighbours to look after the flowers, but we haven't given them a key yet.

5

Have you bought a new picture book for me?
Have you put it in the caravan?
Have you taken away my pencils?
Have you packed my swimming things?
Have you found my red toy car?
Have you put my telephone in the caravan?
Have you seen my teddy?
Have you bought some chocolate?

6

1. *Mrs Mason:* Yes, I have.
2. *Mrs Mason:* Yes, I have.
3. *Kate:* No, I haven't.
4. *All:* Yes, we have.
5. *Timmy:* No, I haven't.
6. *All:* No, we haven't.
7. *Timmy:* No, we can't.

7

Mögliche Fragen:

Have you ever been to a caravan site?	No, I haven't. I have never been to a caravan site.
Have you ever cleaned a caravan?	No, I haven't. I haven't cleaned a caravan yet.
Has your father ever had an accident?	No, he hasn't. He hasn't had an accident yet.
Has your sister ever been to England?	No, she hasn't. She hasn't been to England yet.
Have your friends ever slept in a caravan?	No, they haven't. They have never slept there.

8

1. The Masons have already packed everything.
2. They have given the key of their house to their neighbours.
3. They have put all their things in the caravan.
4. They have left York today.
5. They have already done 100 kilometres.
6. But they have not arrived at their camping site yet.
7. They have all enjoyed their trip so far.
8. They are sure they have never had such a nice trip.
9. Timmy has not been sick again yet.
10. He has not had anything for lunch.
11. But he has already been on his potty four times.

9

Jenny has kissed him goodbye.
He has found them again.
They have packed everything.
Somebody has forgotten to shut it.

Test

1

I have woken up.
I have got out of bed.
I haven't washed.
I have had breakfast.
I have taken my dog for a walk.
I have hurried to school.
I haven't been late.
I have tried to listen.
I haven't made much noise.
I have come here.

2

Mögliche Fragen:
What has happened?
Have you had an accident?
Have you lost your money?
Have you written a bad test?
Have you seen your English teacher?
Have you got up on the wrong side of the bed?
Has your girlfriend left you?
Have you not had/haven't you had breakfast?
Has Sandra tried to kiss you?

3

a) Mike has never been a good worker.
b) He has never liked working.
c) He has always had two left hands.
d) He has nearly never cleaned his room himself.
e) Has he already cleaned his room today?

14 Das *simple past*

1

Regular verbs: visited, tried, laughed, tried, sounded, stopped, laughed
Irregular verbs: did, went, found, had, wasn't

2

Irregular verbs: say, lead, read, buy, write, sit, feel, catch, set, ride, swim, think, feed, leave, fall, meet, fly, let, break, bring, lose, get, teach, pay

3

said, played, carried, flew, bought, caught, fell, stopped, left, thought, let, taught, paid, led, sat, lost, wrote, set, fed, met, read, felt, rode, made, heard, broke

4

Before they left, they checked their car.
They put a good map in it.
They packed their things.
They locked the doors.
They shut the windows.
They switched off all lights.
They said goodbye to their neighbours.
They looked up the route they wanted to take.

5

wanted - was - got - was - wanted - was - knew - was - were -saw - was - got - went - shut - came - wanted - got - carried - were - heard - got - ran - was - arrived - was - were

6

They finally left at 10 o'clock. Their first stop was at 11.30 because Timmy was sick. At 1 o'clock they had lunch, but when they left, they forgot Timmy's teddy. At 2 o'clock they got into their car again and drove on. They arrived at 6 o'clock at the camping site. There they tried to put up a tent for Tom, but it collapsed. They had supper at 8. At 9 they all went to bed because they were very tired.

7

The first night Timmy **did not sleep** very well. He **didn't have** his teddy and it **was** not quiet enough at the camping site. At home he **didn't sleep** in the same bed with Kate. She **didn't leave** him enough room and she **didn't want** him in "her" bed. So Timmy **wasn't** warm enough. He **didn't have** nice dreams and **was not** happy that night.

8

1. Did you sleep well tonight? No, I didn't.
2. Did you miss your teddy?' Yes, I did.
3. Was it quiet enough? No, it wasn't.
4. Did you sleep with all that noise? No, I didn't.
5. Did Kate leave you enough room? No, she didn't.
6. Were you warm enough? No, I wasn't.
7. Did you have nice dreams? No, I didn't.
8. Did you like your first night here? No, I didn't.

9

Lösungsvorschläge:

The first day, they didn't get up early. They had a late breakfast.
Timmy was not sick any more. He felt better.
Tom wrote a letter to Jenny.
Kate looked for new friends.
Mrs Mason didn't do any work.
They didn't stay in the caravan that day.
They didn't lie on the beach, but went for a walk.
They didn't cook in the caravan, but had lunch in a restaurant.

10

Mögliche Fragen:

What's the matter, Kate?
What happened?
How did it happen?
Did anything happen to Timmy?
Did he break anything?
Did he cry?
What did Tom do?
Where is Timmy now?

11

Why didn't Timmy see the stone?
Where did the accident happen?
Did Timmy break his arm?
Did he cry a lot?
How did he look?
Was he sick?
Did they call a doctor?
When did the doctor come?
What did she tell them?
Did Timmy have to go to hospital?

12

- Did it hurt, Timmy?
- How did the accident happen?
- Why didn't you see the stone?
- Did you fall on your arm?
- Did you cry?
- When did you come here?
- Was your teddy all right?
- Who helped you?
- Was anybody with you?

13

1. couldn't
2. had to
3. didn't have to
4. were allowed to
5. couldn't
6. wasn't allowed to
7. was allowed to

14

- He didn't have to make his bed.
- He was allowed to play with his teddy.
- He was allowed to draw pictures with his right arm.
- He didn't have to cook his meals.
- He didn't have to clean the room.
- He didn't have to stay in bed all day.
- He wasn't allowed to play in the corridor.
- He was allowed to look at his picture book.
- He had to be careful with his arm.
- He was allowed to talk to the nurses./He could talk to the nurses.
- He wasn't allowed to run around in the room.
- He wasn't allowed to stand on his right arm.
- He had to eat his meals.
- He had to keep his arm still.

15

Lösungsvorschläge:

Did you have to make your bed? No, I didn't.
Were you allowed to draw pictures with your right arm? Yes, I was.
Did you have to cook your meals? No, I didn't.
Did you have to stay in bed all day? No, I didn't.
Did you have to keep your arm still? Yes, I did.
Were you allowed to look at your picture book? Yes, I was.
Were you allowed to play with your teddy? Yes, I was.
Could you talk to the nurses? Yes, I could.
Were you allowed to run around in the room? No, I wasn't.

Were you allowed to stand on your right arm? No, I wasn't.
Did you have to eat your meals? Yes, I did.
Were you allowed to play in the corridor? No, I wasn't.
Did you have to be careful with your arm? Yes, I did.

16

were allowed – didn't have to – wasn't allowed – didn't have to stay – had to be – wasn't allowed – wasn't allowed – had to take – didn't have to worry – had to look

17

Lösungsvorschläge:

The last time I was ill, I wasn't allowed to go to school. I had to stay in bed all the time. My friends were not allowed to see me …

18

Did you have to go there with your parents?
Did you stay at a hotel?
Did you have to sleep in a tent?
Did you have to take your German books with you?
Were you allowed to stay up late?
When did you have to go to bed?
Did you have to help your parents?
What did you have to do?
Did you make any friends there?
Were there other girls?
Why didn't you kiss them?
Were they nicer than Jenny?
What was the weather like?
Were you happy that you were back?

Test

1

a) I didn't sleep very well.
b) My sister always took my blanket away.
c) She always kicked me.
d) I was very tired, but I couldn't sleep.
e) And it was very cold.
f) Some people were very loud outside.
g) They shouted and played games.
h) I missed my teddy.
i) And I had a bad dream.
j) It was about my teddy.

2

My teddy was all alone in the house. Everybody was gone. He felt very lonely and there were big tears in his eyes. Why had they all left him? … It was dark and dusty there and he couldn't see a thing. And there were noises in the room, noises he didn't know. And they came nearer and nearer. He felt that there was somebody or something watching him. What was it? Suddenly he saw two green eyes and felt something touching him, something that was cold and slimy. He tried to run away, but something kept him back …

3

Where did they go?
What did they enjoy?
Who played a lot of games?
What did Timmy read?
When did they go for long walks?
Where did they go for long walks?
Who did they watch?
What did Mr Mason and Tom do?
What did they tell everybody?

Simple past oder *past progressive*?

1

1. First Tom sent Kate back to their parents.
2. So Kate ran back to the caravan and told her parents all about Timmy's accident.
3. Then Mrs Mason phoned a doctor.
4. When the doctor arrived, she examined Timmy. After that she called an amulance.
5. When the ambulance arrived, the ambulance men put Timmy on a stretcher. Then they carried him inside. After that they drove him to the hospital.

2

Tom and Kate wanted to go to the beach, so I asked Mum if I could go there, too. First she did not want, but then she said yes. So I told Tom to wait for me. I went into the caravan and fetched my teddy. They walked very fast, so I had to run. There was a big stone in my way, but I didn't see it. So I fell over it and broke my arm. I didn't let go my teddy, but held it in my hand. I felt a pain in my leg. Then Tom and Kate came, but I don't know what happened then …

3

Lösungsvorschläge:

When poor Timmy broke his arm,

- his father was smoking and talking,
- his mother was lying in the sun,
- his parents were just having breakfast,
- his parents were just getting up,
- his mother was writing a letter,
- nobody was looking after him.

4

When Timmy had his accident,

- a woman was reading a magazine,
- a man was lying in a deckchair,
- some people were swimming,
- two children were playing with a ball,
- a boy was listening to the radio,
- a girl was putting on her clothes,
- a family was having a picnic.

5

I was playing football when I fell to the ground and broke my arm.

I was climbing a rock when I slipped.

I slipped when I was having a shower.
I broke three ribs.

I was cleaning the windows, when the ladder broke.
I fell onto the floor.

I was lying in my deckchair when it collapsed.

While I was doing my homework, I fell asleep.
I fell off the chair.

6

had to be – couldn't go for a swim – had to keep him busy – often read ghost stories – was – wanted – came – was not shining – was raining – sounded – entered – filled – was – came – saw – heard – opened – saw – fell – were

7

Timmy was lying in his bed. His teddy was sleeping beside him. Suddenly the door opened and somebody came into his room. When he opened his eyes, he saw that a dark figure was standing in front of his bed. It was looking at him. Then it sat down on his bed. A cold hand touched his face. He woke up with a loud cry. The lights went on. His mother was standing in front of him. "Are you dreaming, Timmy?" she said.

Test

1

- The sun was shining. It wasn't raining.
- Some people were playing games.
- Other people were talking to each other.
- People were eating or having something to drink.
- Children were laughing and shouting.
- Some people were swimming in the sea.
- Others were lying in the sun.
- People were putting on their clothes or taking them off.
- Some people were going home.

2

a) When Timmy **came** home, a big surprise **was waiting** for him.
b) A new picture book **was lying** on the table.
c) When Timmy **saw** it, he immediately **opened** it and **began** to "read".

d) While he **was reading**, his parents **unpacked** his things.
e) When they **came** back, Timmy **was sleeping**.
f) Mr Mason **took** him in his arms and **carried** him upstairs into his room.
g) There he **put** him in his bed.
h) Timmy **did** not **wake** up; he **was dreaming** of doctors, ghosts and other things.

Simple past und *present perfect* 16

1

1. We came back yesterday.
2. I often went swimming.
3. I met Mike in the holidays.
4. I got to know a German boy.
5. I talked a lot of German.
6. We had an accident.
7. I didn't do any homework in the holidays.
8. I ate too much in the holidays.
9. I have become really fat.
10. We visited a lot of castles in the holidays.

2

In the holidays we visited Carisbrooke Castle. Carisbrooke Castle is an old castle. It is famous, too, because Charles I was a prisoner there ... People say that he hasn't found peace yet and that his ghost is still walking there.
When we came there, the sky was very dark. When we walked through the entrance, it began to rain. So we went into the castle, but it was very dark in there, too. There were lots of strange noises. Suddenly a door opened. When I looked there, I saw something green. It was coming towards me. I ran out of the building and told everything to my parents. They didn't believe me. They just laughed at me.
After the holidays were over, we had to go home again. The first night I went to bed early, but woke up at midnight. There was a strange noise again. I saw something green. It was sitting at my desk and was writing something in an exercise book. I was very afraid and did not move. Five minutes later it was gone. I got up and went to the desk. There I saw my German exercise book. It was open and there was a note in the book. It ran: ... This is what the ghost told me and that's why I did not do any homework last Tuesday.

3

This was our hotel. We stayed there for two weeks.
We always went swimming there.
We had an accident. We haven't repaired our car yet.
We visited the castle. Did you know that Charles I was a prisoner here? I played with him a lot. We often went to the beach and had a swim together.
And that girl over there is his sister. We played with her sometimes.

4

1. When did you come back?
2. Where did you go?
3. Did you like your stay there?
4. Have you ever been to Italy?
5. Did you do anything for school as our teacher told you?
6. Did you play tennis in the holidays?
7. How many postcards did you write?
8. Where did you buy these shoes?
9. What was the weather like? Did it rain a lot?
10. Have you already seen Mike?

5

Mögliche Antworten:

I couldn't do my homework because
- my neighbour was ill.
- I left my book at school.
- my mother/father/sister was ill yesterday.
- I felt so ill in the afternoon.
- my pen did not work.
- I forgot my school bag.
- my exercise book was full.
- I had to repair my bike.
- my mother had no time to help me.
- I couldn't open my school bag.
- my printer didn't work.
- my computer broke down.

I can't show you my homework because
- I have left it on the bus/at home.
- I have forgotten my school bag.
- my baby brother/sister has ruined it.
- my baby brother made a plane out of it.
- somebody has stolen it.

Test

1

a) I put the luggage in the car.
b) Then we all got into the car.
c) We had to stop at a traffic light.
d) Somebody crashed/bumped into our car.
e) We all got out of the car.
f) Nobody was injured.
g) But our car was damaged.
h) Then we had to wait for the police and couldn't drive on.

2

Tom:

Did you get my letters?/**Have you got** my the letters? I **wrote** the last one two days ago. But tell me, when **did you come** back? How **did you like** London?

Jenny:

I **got** your other letters, but I **haven't got** last one yet. How many letters **did you write**? I **came** back two days ago.

Well, I **liked** it, but my aunt **was** terrible sometimes. She just **thought** that I was a small baby. She always **said** that I **was** too young to look after myself. And she **didn't like** your letters, Tom.

Didn't she like my handwriting?

Adjektive 17

1

Mögliche Antworten:

My friend? He is tall and thin, but he is very strong, too.
My friend? She is fat and small, but she is exciting, too.
My sister? She is nice and funny, but she can be difficult, too.
My brother? He noisy and fat, but he but he can be nice, too.
...

2

Mögliche Antworten:

The boy/girl I'd like to meet should be clever/intelligent/interesting/funny ...
He/she shouldn't be boring/difficult/stupid ...
My dream boy/dream girl should be intelligent/funny/nice ...

3

Mögliche Antworten:

Comics are boring/interesting/wonderful/exciting/fantastic ...
Films are boring/funny/interesting/exciting/wonderful ...
Books are interesting/exciting/wonderful/fantastic/funny...
Football is exciting/boring/fantastic/dangerous/interesting/difficult ...
TV is boring/bad/exciting/fantastic/dangerous/interesting ...
English tests are wonderful/fantastic/exciting/funny/interesting ...
Boys are exciting/dangerous/wonderful/clever/intelligent ...
Teachers are loud/boring/dangerous/strange/crazy ...

Baby brothers/sisters are loud/fat/noisy/boring ...
Pop music is beautiful/fantastic/wonderful/loud ...

4

a funny girl	– a boring girl
an old town	– a new/modern town
a small boy	– a tall boy
a good mark	– a bad mark
a boring film	– an interesting/an exciting film
a fast runner	– a slow runner
a bad driver	– a good driver
a slow worker	– a fast worker
a clever pupil	– a silly pupil
a quiet boy	– a noisy boy
a happy child	– an unhappy child
a difficult test	– an easy test
a silly person	– a clever/an intelligent person
a terrible story	– a nice story
a rich man	– a poor man
a dirty room	– a clean room

5

bad, worse, the worst; beautiful, more beautiful, the most beautiful; good, better, the best; boring, more boring, the most boring; busy, busier, the busiest; careful, more careful, the most careful; crazy, crazier, the craziest; exciting, more exciting, the most exciting; fantastic, more fantastic, the most fantastic; noisy, noisier, the noisiest; fat, fatter, the fattest; loud, louder, the loudest; modern, more modern, the most modern; poor, poorer, the poorest; powerful, more powerful, the most powerful; quick, quicker, the quickest; slow, slower, the slowest; strange, stranger, the strangest; tall, taller, the tallest; small, smaller, the smallest; thin, thinner, the thinnest; strong, stronger, the strongest; worried, more worried, the most worried; nice, nicer, the nicest; clever, cleverer, the cleverest; intelligent, more intelligent, the most intelligent; funny, funnier, the funniest; heavy, heavier, the heaviest; dangerous, more dangerous, the most dangerous, interesting, more interesting, the most interesting; wonderful, more wonderful, the most wonderful; difficult, more difficult, the most difficult

6

Mögliche Antworten:

Tom's dad is the tallest in the family. He is taller than Grandpa and he is taller than Mum/his wife. Tom is the tallest of the children. Kate and Timmy are smaller than Tom. Timmy is the smallest of them all.

7

Susan: I think tennis is more difficult than swimming.
Betty: No, it isn't, but it's more expensive.
Susan: More expensive? I think swimming is as expensive as tennis.
Susan: I think English is nicer than German.
Betty: No, it isn't, but it's more useful.
Susan: More useful? I think it's as useful as English.
Susan: I think comics are funnier than books.
Betty: No, they aren't, but books are more interesting than comics.
Susan: More interesting? I think comics are as interesting as books.

8

… I think he's **the tallest** boy in our class.
… No, I think David is **taller than** him.
… He must be **the strongest** boy …
… He is even **nicer** than Tom.
… It has got the same colour **as** your hair.
… or you'll get a prize for **the silliest** question.
… I need somebody who is **cleverer than** Tom. You know, at maths Tom is even **worse than** me.
… He looks a bit silly, but perhaps he is **better** at maths **than** he looks.
… Anne told me his photos are **the best** photos she has ever seen.
… Then they must be **good**. She always thinks she's **the nicest** girl in our class.

9

1. Has your English become **better**?
2. Let's hope it hasn't become **worse**.
3. Is the number of mistakes in your English tests **smaller** or **bigger** than before?
4. Were the exercises very **boring**?
5. Were they **more interesting** than in your textbook?
6. Were they **as boring as** in your textbook?
7. Or were they **worse**?
8. Was the grammar **clear** enough?
9. Or was the grammar in your textbook **easier**?
10. We hope that you didn't find things too **difficult**.

Test

1

a) York is one of the **oldest** cities in England.
b) It was, together with London, the **most important** town in Roman times.
c) York has many monuments. It has … the **largest** medieval Cathedral in Northern Europe.
d) The Jorvic Viking Centre is one of the **most interesting** museums …
e) It is the **biggest** railway museum in the world.
f) It offers one of the **most beautiful** sights in Northern England.

2

a) New York is much **bigger than** York.
b) York's population isn't **as mixed as** New York's population.
c) York is much **older than** New York.
d) New York's history isn't **as old as** York's, but it's certainly **as interesting**.
e) New York's climate is different. It's much **hotter** in summer and much **colder** in winter.
f) There is more money in New York today **than** in York. Most people are **richer**, but there are also many people who are **poorer**.

18 Adverbien

1

1. She dances **well**.
2. He runs **fast**.
3. She sings **beautifully**.
4. She does everything **quietly**.
5. He always runs around **noisily**.
6. She works **hard**.
7. She always answers **cleverly**.
8. He always laughs **happily**.
9. She dances **terribly**.
10. He speaks German **very well**.

2

Lösungsvorschläge:

a) I can speak English very well. I also play football very well. I am a good worker and do my homework very carefully. My teachers think that I'm very intelligent; I always answer cleverly and do things intelligently. I understand things easily, too.

b) My friend is a bit slow. He does everything very slowly, but he does things carefully. He doesn't speak English very well, but he is very good at maths. He often writes very badly, so I can't read it very easily. Sometimes he is a bit boring, but he sings wonderfully.

3

quietly – silly – thick – red – excited – quiet – angrily – afraid – quickly – slowly – good – carefully – quickly – ready – slowly – sure

4

1. Lots of windows were still **open**.
2. Some pupils were running around **excitedly** …
3. Others were still **quietly** packing their things.
4. One pupil was **busily** copying his homework … He wasn't even writing very **fast**.
5. He didn't think it was **dangerous** to remain in the building.
6. Some were **excitedly** watching the smoke …
7. Others were **happy** that there was a fire at their school.
8. A **good** fire is less **boring** than an English lesson, one of them said **excitedly**.
9. And there will be no English tomorrow, somebody else added **quickly**.

5

Lösungsvorschläge:

1. Four men jumped out of it **quickly**.
2. Two of them ran into the building **quickly**.
3. They **busily** raised a ladder.
4. One man **carefully** climbed up the ladder.
5. Another man **quickly** fetched the water hose.
6. "Where can we take the water from?" one man asked **nervously/worriedly**.
7. "Where do we begin?" one man asked **nervously**.

Test

1

a) When there is a fire, don't be **nervous**, don't run around **excitedly**, but keep cool and pack your things **quickly**.
b) Shut all windows and doors **carefully** … leave the room as **fast** as you can.
c) … try **hard** not to get excited.
d) Follow the instructions of the firemen **carefully**.
e) Make a **good** job out of a **bad** thing.

2

Mögliche Antworten:

a) I was quietly sitting in the classroom … I quickly understood the danger we were in.
b) … managed to put out the fire quickly.
c) Teachers and pupils were running around fast/excitedly/nervously.
d) There were quite a lot of pupils who behaved stupidly.
e) I quickly ran along the corridor with the other pupils of my class; we loudly shouted …
f) My neighbour coughed badly when the smoke got into his lungs.

19 Die Wortstellung im Englischen

1

On Monday, I am going to play table tennis with Tom at 4 p.m.
On Tuesday, I am going to watch a film on TV at 8.15 p.m.
On Wednesday, I am going to learn for a German test with Tom after school.
On Thursday, I am going to help Kate with her maths homework at 6 p.m.
On Friday, I am going to buy a birthday present for Sarah at 5 p.m.; then I am going to ring her up.
On Saturday, I am going to go to Sarah's birthday party at 2 p.m.
On Sunday, I am going to ring up Tom and go for a walk with him at 4 p.m.

2

1. Today I am ill.
2. Today I needn't get up.
3. Today I can stay in bed.
4. Today I needn't go to school.
5. Today I needn't do any homework.
6. Today I have got no German.
7. Today I have got a temperature.
8. Today is a beautiful day.

3

Did I give **it to you**, Christine?
Perhaps you gave **it to** Sandra.
Can any of you lend **me** some money?
I've already lent **some to** Tom.
You can have your chips and bring **me your money** tomorrow.
I won't forget to give **it** back **to** you.

4

There are pupils
- who usually forget their homework.
- who have never forgotten their homework.
- who often do their homework at school.
- who have never copied it from their neighbours.
- who never know what they must do.
- who never write down what they must do.
- who always forget their homework at home.
- who usually do it on the way to school.
- who sometimes leave their exercise book at home.
- who sometimes forget it on the bus.

5

Mögliche Antworten:

1. I usually do my homework/Yes, I do.
2. I usually/always do it in the afternoon/in the evening/in the morning.
3. I usually do it at home/on the bus/at school.
4. I don't usually forget it/No, I don't.
5. I sometimes forget it when I have got no time/when I don't think of it.
6. I never copy it from my neighbour/No, never. I only sometimes copy it from him/her.
7. No, I'm not. I usually play with my neighbour or talk to him/her.
8. No, they needn't. They needn't often help me/Yes, they must. They must often help me.
9. He/she must often help me in …
10. Yes, he/she has/No, he/she hasn't. He/she has never helped me.

6

1. English pupils already go to school when they are five.
2. Most English pupils go to a comprehensive school when they are eleven.

3. They can leave school when they are 16.
4. In many schools they must wear school uniforms.
5. The school colours in Tom's school are blue and grey.
6. The pupils' parents can buy the school uniforms in special shops.
7. In most English schools lessons begin later than in Germany.
8. Most English pupils also have lessons in the afternoon.
9. There are lessons also in the afternoon, so many English schools have school cafeterias.
10. Pupils can have lunch in the school cafeteria during lunch break.
11. In many English schools pupils learn to cook.

7

Mögliche Antworten:

Before I go to school, I usually do my homework.
When I don't want to go to school, I tell my mum that I am ill.
When it's too cold to get up, I stay in bed.
When I am late, I don't have breakfast.
When I must do my homework, I ask my friend to help me.
When I must go to bed, I still read an hour or two.
Before I get up, I often think that it is too early to get up.
Before I have breakfast, I usually wash.
When I go to bed, I switch off the lights.
When I can't find my homework, I get angry.

Test

1

a) Today I'll play football. I usually play football on Fridays.
b) On Mondays, I sometimes go to the cinema.
c) After school, I often go to Tom.
d) What we do there? We usually play games or do our homework.
e) No, we seldom play with Kate.
f) When I'm at home, I often watch TV.
g) Yes, I usually do.
h) If my parents are often out? … sometimes they are and sometimes they aren't.
i) I always go to bed at 10.
j) I usually get up at 7.
k) If I'm often late? I'm never late.

2

a) As you know, German schools are different from English schools.
b) Pupils usually start school at the age of 6 or 7.
c) In Germany lessons start earlier than in England.
d) In most cases German schools are no all-day schools.
e) German pupils usually have lunch at home.
f) Most German schools have no school cafeterias.
g) So German pupils don't spend so much time at school.
h) They usually are at home in the early afternoon.

Notwendige Relativsätze 20

1

1. A pilot is somebody who flies a plane.
2. A nurse is a woman who looks after people who are ill.
3. A doctor is somebody who examines sick people.
4. A vet is somebody who looks after sick animals.
5. A shopkeeper is somebody who has got a shop
6. A shop assistant is somebody who works in a shop.
7. A car mechanic is somebody who repairs cars.
8. A customer is somebody who buys things.
9. A mother is a woman who has children.
10. A bus driver is somebody who drives a bus.

2

Mögliche Lösungen:
A girl is somebody who talks a lot.
A teenager is somebody who isn't a baby anymore.
A test is something which can be a problem.
A pupil is somebody who is lazy and loud.
School is something that makes you learn a lot of silly things.
A teacher is somebody who talks a lot.
A school report is something which makes my parents cry.
A mother is somebody who asks too many questions.
A bad mark is something that makes you sad.

3

1. Tom hasn't got a real hobby, but there are many things he likes.
2. He likes school, but he doesn't like all the subjects he must take.
3. Mike likes girls, but he doesn't like all the girls who are in his class.
4. Kate likes sleeping. Her bed is the piece of furniture she likes best.
5. Jenny likes pets. The pet she has got is a hamster.
6. Her friend likes pop music. She collects all the CDs she can buy.
7. Timmy likes picture books. He can colour all the pictures he sees in them.
8. Mike likes taking photos.He puts the photos he has taken in an album, too.
9. John likes food. The food which is on his plate looks good.
10. Mr Mason likes working on the farm he has got.

Test

1

1. A pupil is somebody who still goes to school.
2. A classmate is somebody who is in your class.
3. A test is something which can be a problem.
4. A monster is somebody who looks like my teacher.
5. A game is something which can be very funny.
6. A vegetarian is somebody doesn't eat any meat.
7. Football is something which can be very interesting.

2

Do you like all the pupils who are in your class?
Are there any girls you like?
Are there any pupils you can't stand?
Are there any pupils who don't like you?
Are there any pupils who are afraid of you?
Is there anything you do together after school?
Are there any games you play together?
What are the games you like best?

3

1. Jenny is the girl Tom likes best.
2. Most of the other boys and girls who are in her class like her, too.
3. There are only few people who don't like her.
4. The teachers who know her like her, too.